Praise for *The Essential Guide*

"As Margaret shares in her amazing book, *Essential Guide* ..., we are not alone. We have lots of help. In fact, there is an angel to assist us with actualizing every desire. This is the most important book you can ever employ—daily—to create a wondrous life. Every tool is explained, including which colors, gemstones, and affirmations will summon an everyday angel to support your dreams and wishes."

—Cyndi Dale, author of *Energy Healing for Trauma, Stress & Chronic Conditions*

"*The Essential Guide to Everyday Angels* is an inspirational, informative, and practical book on how to work with your angels to achieve success in every area of your life. It's essential reading for anyone seeking to establish or maintain a close connection with the angelic realms. This is an important book that teaches powerful practices in Margaret Ann Lembo's usual readable style. Highly recommended."

—Richard Webster, author of *Spirit Guides & Angel Guardians*

"Margaret's lovely teachings shine the light on the angelic realms. She demonstrates how our thoughts and petitions help connect you to angels. Allow their presence to help guide you on your path."

—Amy Zerner and Monte Farber, bestselling authors of *The Enchanted Tarot, The Truth Fairy,* and *The Creativity Oracle*

THE ESSENTIAL GUIDE

to

EVERYDAY

Angels

© Forever Studios

About the Author

Margaret Ann Lembo is the author of *Chakra Awakening; The Essential Guide to Crystals, Minerals and Stones; The Essential Guide to Aromatherapy and Vibrational Healing; The Angels & Gemstone Guardians Cards; Gemstone Guardians Cards & Your Soul Purpose*, many more decks, and nine spoken audio CDs. She is the creator of a line of award-winning Aroma-Energetic Sprays, including Smudge in Spray™, and over fifty aromatic blends. She is a spiritual entrepreneur, an evolutionary aromatherapist, and the owner of The Crystal Garden, the Conscious Living Store and Center of the Palm Beaches, established in 1988.

THE ESSENTIAL GUIDE

to

EVERYDAY

Angels

Llewellyn Publications
Woodbury, Minnesota

MARGARET ANN LEMBO

FIRST EDITION
First Printing, 2020

Book design by Samantha Penn
Cover design by Shira Atakpu
Chakra figure on page 8 by Mary Ann Zapalac

Llewellyn Publications is a registered trademark of Llewellyn Worldwide Ltd.

Library of Congress Cataloging-in-Publication Data
Names: Lembo, Margaret Ann, author.
Title: The essential guide to everyday angels / Margaret Ann Lembo.
Description: First edition. | Woodbury, Minnesota : Llewellyn Publications,
    [2020] | Includes bibliographical references and index. | Summary: "The
    Essential Guide to Everyday Angels shares tips and techniques so you can
    connect to angels for more than fifty specific needs, from abundance to
    unconditional love" —Provided by publisher.
Identifiers: LCCN 2020019290 (print) | LCCN 2020019291 (ebook) | ISBN
    9780738764993 (paperback) | ISBN 9780738765143 (ebook)
Subjects: LCSH: Angels—Miscellanea.
Classification: LCC BF1623.A53 L46 2020 (print) | LCC BF1623.A53 (ebook)
    | DDC 202/.15—dc23
LC record available at https://lccn.loc.gov/2020019290
LC ebook record available at https://lccn.loc.gov/2020019291

Llewellyn Publications
A Division of Llewellyn Worldwide Ltd.
2143 Wooddale Drive
Woodbury, MN 55125-2989
www.llewellyn.com

Printed in the United States of America

Other Books by Margaret Ann Lembo

The Angels & Gemstone Guardians Cards
The Animal Allies & Gemstone Guardians Cards
Animal Totems and the Gemstone Kingdom
The Archangels & Gemstone Guardians Cards
Chakra Awakening
Color Your Life with Crystals
Color Your Life with Good Thoughts: A Coloring Book
Crystals Beyond Beginners
Crystal Intentions Oracle
The Essential Guide to Aromatherapy and Vibrational Healing
The Essential Guide to Crystals, Minerals, and Stones
Gemstone Guardians Cards & Your Soul Purpose
Masters, Mystics, Saints & Gemstone Guardians Cards

Forthcoming Books by Margaret Ann Lembo

The Essential Guide to Archangels and Saints

To my sister, Mary Ann,
who taught me to imagine, know, and visualize
angels all around me when I was a little girl.

Disclaimer

I do not recommend or endorse the internal use of essential oils. The uses described within these pages include inhalation and topical use only. Most oils should not be used during pregnancy or nursing, and all are generally contraindicated during the first trimester or while nursing. Many should not be used on children under the age of six.

For ages six and under, the safest dilution rate is 0.25 percent dilution. For ages over six, the typical dilution is 1 percent. For example, if you were to use six drops of essential oil in twenty mL of a carrier oil for an adult, then for a child over age six, you would use one drop to 100 mL of carrier oil.

Always practice essential oil safety. Remember to use a carrier oil when applying essential oils to your skin. Any oils that have gone rancid should be discarded.

Check on the contraindications in the "for your safety" section under each essential oil in my book *The Essential Guide to Aromatherapy and Vibrational Healing* to ensure you have a pleasant experience. For instance, some oils lower your blood pressure (clary sage, sweet marjoram, ylang-ylang, etc.), which may be beneficial for those with high blood pressure but may be harmful for those with low blood pressure.

CONTENTS

INTRODUCTION

*F*or as long as I can remember, angels have been part of my daily life. As a child, I felt and saw them in my imagination and called on their help whenever I was afraid or needed guidance. It was normal to imagine an angel, or a group of angels, surrounding me while I slept, ate, walked to school, took tests, and did all the things we do as children. This foundation of knowing that everyday angels were always available and at my side has helped me have a much happier and spiritual life. These core beliefs, established in childhood, are important factors in the spiritually focused woman I have become.

My sister, Mary Ann, was instrumental in helping me realize that I have angels all around me to help me. We shared a room and when I'd wake up in the night afraid, Mary Ann would comfort me and tell me to imagine my angels all around me, watching over me while I slept. I am so grateful that I acquired this practice and knowledge at an early age.

I still actively connect with my angelic helpers for everyday life situations. Growing up in an Italian Roman Catholic family, it was common and normal in home and at school to make room for my guardian angel at my desk or at the dinner table or in any type of life situation. To this day, I intuitively hear and know that I have an entourage of angels, or sometimes legions of angels, at my beck and call. It is as simple as having a thought, imagining the angels around me, and then having faith that my heavenly helpers are "on the job" so I can relax and allow life to unfold.

Since the early 1990s I have presented many talks and workshops at bookstores throughout the US and in Canada with the intention of helping people connect with their angels. These heavenly messengers are waiting for instructions from each and every one of us. The telepathic assistance from the angelic realm is a very real part of my life; it can easily become a very real part of your life and make your life much easier.

As my knowledge of and love for crystals, minerals, and stones grew, I became aware of the various vibrational matches available through the energy of working with colorful gems. The angels are beings of light, each of them associated with a color or range of colors. Therefore, gemstones are perfect reminders to maintain a focus on intended goals and aspirations because the gemstones resonate with the color or ray of the angels and archangels, too. Tying the angelic world to crystals, minerals, and stones helps ground the connection I have with the angelic realm and will for you too.

My desire for using all six senses to increase my awareness and awaken consciousness has led me to use essential oils to honor my olfactory senses. To smell the essence of everyday angels surrounding me helps make the angels even more real and palpable. I consider myself an evolutionary aromatherapist because the blends that I've created are divinely inspired with the intention of helping people transform their life. The blends I've created in association with spiritual beings are tools, just like gemstones, to help you maintain your focus on your goals and aspirations. You'll read more about these blends in appendix B of this book under aromatherapy resources.

Throughout my life I've practiced the use of affirmations. I find them extremely powerful. When I first started practicing affirmations, I'd write them in my journals. I have used index cards and sticky notes throughout my home, car, and offices to help me remember that I create my reality through focus and action. The affirmation on my desk right now as I write this paragraph is, "I have plenty of time and space to do all that I want to do and plenty of time to do all that I need to do." This affirmation has helped me relax into knowing this truth. Enjoy practicing the affirmations that you will find throughout this book.

Talking with angels is easy. Simply imagine their energy standing or sitting near you as they listen to what you are feeling, fearing, and hoping. Use your imagination and activate your ability to make believe. Hold a gemstone and inhale an aroma to amplify the angelic interaction experience. Then tell the angels how you would like their help and support. Drawing inspiration from this book, formulate what you want so you can clearly express your request for assistance. Be as clear and specific as possible, then consider adding this statement, "May this or something better become manifest reality."

These pages will guide you through getting to know your own personal angels and encourage you to use them. They are waiting for instructions. Angels aren't able to intervene until you specifically request their help with detailed instructions on how you want them to help you. Throughout this book you will garner ideas on how to connect and request assistance.

Angels All Around

Angels are luminous beings of light emanating from God, the Divine.

Whether or not you are conscious of them, you have *many* invisible helpers around you every moment of your life. Imagine them there or just know that a large group of invisible helpers are ready to come to your aid. They're watching over you, inspiring you, and guiding you along your path through life. They're with you 24/7: when you are sleeping and when you are awake. And they're just a thought away when you're ready to be conscious of them. Angels have a high vibration and provide energetic assistance to us upon request. The personalities and qualities of these spiritual beings bring a plethora of positive vibes to your spiritual table.

Angels and archangels are androgynous, neither masculine nor feminine. While humankind has personified them to look like humans with wings and flowing robes, they are actually beings of light, color, and vibration. Angels act and react based on the thoughts of their human charges. They respond to prayers, requests, and petitions. They act as Divine messengers, communicating guidance and wisdom as well as the orchestration of synchronicity. They are focused on Divine will and the highest good of all concerned.

Archangels are messenger angels of high rank. They are beings of love and light with designated responsibilities to guide and assist us here on Earth. Despite their masculine- or feminine-sounding names, they are genderless light beings. They are available to help us when invoked or petitioned for a specific purpose in alignment with the Divine plan.

There are many archangels, and you'll find them listed throughout this book as additional support for specific reasons. Whenever you want to know more about a certain archangel, you can look in appendix A. The four main archangels, Michael, Raphael, Gabriel, and Uriel, are familiar to many, but let me introduce you to them.

Archangel Michael is the archangel to call on when you feel you need protection. He is most often portrayed with a sword of light that he uses to slay fears, phobias, negative energy, and obsessions. Michael's energy is cobalt or electric blue.

Archangel Raphael is the angel of healing. Call on Raphael when you need guidance on how to heal yourself or others and to inspire you to find the perfect health-care practitioners. He is said to be the head of the Guardian Angels. Raphael's energy is emerald green.

Archangel Gabriel is the angel well known for the Annunciation; he brought the message to Mother Mary that she would be the woman to bring Jesus Christ into the world. Call on Gabriel for inspiration and guidance and to help you with your intuition and inner knowing. Gabriel is helpful for dream interpretation too. Gabriel's color is red.

Archangel Uriel is the archangel that helps you connect with inner wisdom and peace. Uriel is also the angel of natural phenomena and storms—hail, fire, thunder, hurricanes, volcanoes, earthquakes—and is the guide to help humans be a good steward of the earth. Uriel's color is gold.

You can align with the archangels every day and night until it becomes a habit. Visualize and imagine Archangel Michael before you, Archangel Raphael behind you, Archangel Gabriel on your left side, Archangel Uriel on your right side, and your Guardian Angel above you. Don't worry too much about who is where, but do invite all five of those angels to aid you in changing and shifting your reality to one of inner peace, harmony, and love. Imagine a strong connection of roots of white light from the soles of your feet into the ever-loving Mother Earth. Know and believe you are divinely protected.

In this book you will learn about the most common angels of light, color, and vibration and how to work and play with them to create a happy, balanced life. The angelic realm is waiting for you to give them permission to help and needs specific requests to activate their assistance. Because humans have free will, angels need to be asked to assist us or intervene on our behalf. They respond to thoughts and "hear" what you are thinking if you want them to help. To gain angelic assistance, simply think of the type of assistance you need or want. Determine the area of life to which it pertains. Then ask the everyday angel to guide you and inspire you to achieve that goal or intention. Use the recommended gemstones, essential oils, colors, and affirmations until you realize that your request has been answered.

If you aren't focused on the petitions, affirmations, or aromas, it could symbolize that you've integrated your request into your life and can move forward with your focus on another area of your life. You will notice that you are no longer drawn to carry your gems with you or that you stopped saying the associated affirmations as often.

Petitions and Prayers

Petitions, which are a form of prayer, are earnest requests for something to happen, transform, or change. These petitions are addressed to the angels assigned to a particular area of life. It is very effective to invite God to be the main recipient of your petition with the specific angels as additional address-ees. After all, angels are messengers between humans and God.

Some petitions are made in writing. Though it isn't necessary to put your prayer requests in writing, the act of writing the petition to a specific group of angels often helps clarify and delineate the actions needed to achieve a goal or state of being. Written petitions are effectively created in letter for-mat. Additionally, your thoughts and the action of writing brings the request closer to manifest reality. To bring your request into manifest reality means that your words and thoughts become real in the physical, mental, emo-tional, and spiritual sense.

Manifesting is the active form of prayer. Asking the angels to be part of your team as co-creators and helpers adds a level of conscious awareness to your intention to align with the Divine—God. Meditation and inquiry are considered passive forms of prayer—to sit, to wait, to listen, and to grow.

How to Use This Book

In the upcoming pages, you will discover the names or titles assigned to the luminous beings of light who are patiently waiting for your permission to assist you with living here on Earth. Each angel is described along with their associated chakra, color, gemstone, and scent. These associations are adjunct tools that help you amplify your prayer or petition (the reason you are calling on the angel) by helping you stay focused and clear on the desired outcome. To keep the doorways to heavenly higher consciousness open and flowing, always maintain an intention of "this or something better will manifest." Use the suggested petition or let the petition inspire you to create your own. Repeat the affirmation associated with each angel to help amplify the potential for a positive outcome.

Here is an outline to get you started in your relationship with your angels:

1. Identify the angel or angels you want to work and play with for your given intention.

2. Write a petition to those chosen angels. Keep it simple and concise. You will find a suggested petition for each of the everyday angels included in this book.

3. Keep one or more of the recommended gemstones nearby while you write and during the upcoming days, weeks, or months of manifestation.

4. Use essential oils with the indicated scents or aromatic notes to activate your olfactory senses. This will further assist you in recognizing the realization of the requested action. There is an additional list of aromatherapy blends available in appendix B.

5. Wear one or more of the suggested colors that match the angel(s) on duty.

6. Visualize and imagine the requested everyday angels starting the process. Your imagination is one of the biggest keys to success. Repeatedly use the affirmation provided to help your intention to manifest.

7. Invite the supportive archangels to help you in achieving your goals and intentions. These archangels have a specific energy or "job description" and can add quite a bit of angelic assistance to you as

you work with the everyday angels to design your reality and transform your life. Refer to appendix A in the back of this book to get to know the specific archangels and how they can help you.

The world of imagination is the foundation and core for the manifestation of anything your heart desires. Imagine your life as if a certain situation already exists, and it will be so in very short order because whatever you put your attention on becomes a reality. Mindfulness and awareness of thoughts, words, and feelings are the keys to consciously creating circumstances.

The everyday angels are your entourage. In this setting *you* are the important person, and these designated angels are your personal bodyguards and team players! Delegate and direct your team to assist you in achieving your goals and dreams. They will pave the way to creating the life you want and deserve.

Following the name of the everyday angel is a series of self-inquiry questions. It is the first step in getting to know yourself. Self-knowledge is key to awakening your awareness and aids with mindfulness, the state of being present in each moment. These self-inquiry questions are also a form of affirmations posed as questions that you don't need to answer. Rather, allow them to swirl in your consciousness and subconsciousness and out into the universe until answers naturally come forward.

A description of the everyday angel's "job" or purpose follows the self-inquiry questions. These descriptions will help you figure out when and why you might want to call on a particular angel to light your path. They will guide you and provide inspiration for ease in that area of your life.

Chakras

For each everyday angel, you will see the chakras associated with them and their life area. Chakras are listed as recommendations for focus and awakening your awareness on a spiritual, mental, emotional, and/or spiritual level. Contemplate how you relate to the chakra of the particular everyday angel you are working with in order to deepen your spiritual awareness.

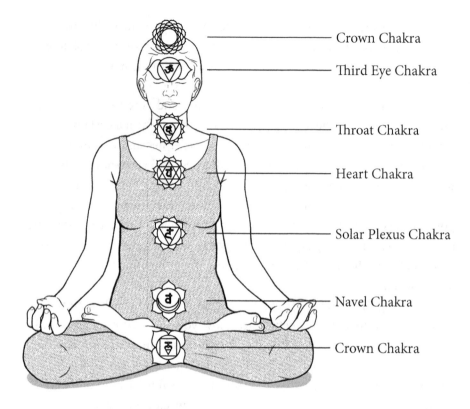

Crown Chakra

Third Eye Chakra

Throat Chakra

Heart Chakra

Solar Plexus Chakra

Navel Chakra

Crown Chakra

Here is a short overview of the chakra system. You can read more about chakras in my article "Chakras and Colorful Healing Gems, Stones, and Minerals" for *Retailing Insight Magazine*.

Root Chakra

Color: Red

The foundation of your physical nature is located here, which includes basic survival needs like food, shelter, and water. The root chakra also includes financial success, abundance, and physical vitality. Motivation, focus, and grounding are key elements of this chakra.

Navel Chakra

Color: Orange

This is sometimes called the sacral chakra. Creativity, the ability to take action and manifest, and your gut feelings of intuition reside here. This is the center where your energy gives birth to your reality.

Solar Plexus Chakra

Color: Yellow

Self-esteem and the courage to live up to your full potential are key for this chakra. Digestion of food and the digestion of life are important aspects of the energy here.

Heart Chakra

Colors: Green and pink

Love, kindness, tolerance, and compassion are the main focus of the heart chakra. This chakra is the bridge that brings heaven to Earth and your connection with blessings and well-being.

Throat Chakra

Color: Light blue or turquoise

Communication is the main focus of the throat chakra. It encompasses your ability to express yourself, be heard, and to listen well. This center helps you align with intuition and Divine timing.

Third Eye Chakra

Color: Indigo

The third eye, located in the center of your brain, is the place of intuition and the ability to pay attention to your inner knowing.

Crown Chakra

Colors: White, gold, and purple

Mental clarity, spiritual connection, and your personal connection with the Divine is the energy of this chakra.

Colors

Use the color that is a vibrational match for the everyday angel and area of life. Wearing these colors and using them in other ways helps you stay focused on being conscious and aware that you are working with that angel on a given situation. Let the color be a reminder for mindfulness: reestablish your intention every time you look at the color of your clothing or placement of a particular color. The use of color as a tool for focus will assist you in maintaining your attention on what you want to achieve instead of what you don't want in your life.

Gemstones

Use the suggested crystals and gemstones as a sparkling tool to stay focused on your intentions and petitions to the everyday angels. In order for the gems to be effective, be sure to establish an intention that matches the reason you are calling on a particular everyday angel. There are many ways to incorporate gems in your daily life. Place one or more of the suggested gemstones in your pocket or on your desk. Wear the crystals and gemstones in jewelry or decorative accessories to amplify your constant focus and attention. Place a crystal grid or create a little altar with gemstones as a reminder of your intended goal.

Read more about the various ways to use crystals, minerals, and stones in your daily life in one of my books. See the "other books by" section in the front of this book to find out more.

Essential Oils

Included with the entry for each everyday angel, you will find suggested essential oils to awaken your awareness and amplify your focus on your ultimate outcome. When you apply or diffuse the suggested essential oils, you are engaging your olfactory nerve and signaling to your brain and body that you are in the process of manifesting your intentions with the help of the angelic assistance you have requested. By engaging the limbic system of your brain (the part that deals with emotion and memory) with the scent, you are establishing another tool for mindful thinking.

Always use essential oils in alignment with established aromatherapy guidelines. Professional organizations such as the National Association of Holistic Aromatherapy (NAHA) and the International Federation of Professional Aromatherapists (IFPA) post safety considerations and guidelines on their websites for the use of essential oils in all circumstances. More resources to understand how to safely use essential oils are provided in appendix B in the back of this book.

The uses described within these pages include inhalation and topical use only. Always practice essential oil safety, and remember to use the essential oil with a base oil when applying it to your skin. I do not recommend or endorse the internal use of essential oils. Any oils that have gone rancid should be discarded. Check on the contraindications in the "for your safety" sections in my book *The Essential Guide to Aromatherapy and Vibrational Healing* to ensure you have a pleasant experience. For instance, some oils like clary sage, sweet marjoram, and ylang-ylang lower your blood pressure, which may be beneficial for those with high blood pressure but may be harmful for those with low blood pressure.

Supportive Archangels

The archangels associated with each of the everyday angels add another layer of spiritual connection. Archangels are messenger angels of high rank. They have specific qualities that they use while helping with your current life challenge or request for assistance. Archangels are able to help you upon request. You must ask for their guidance. Be as specific as possible as they are around you to assist you here on Earth. They are available to help you when petitioned for a specific purpose in alignment with the Divine plan. More about the archangels can be found in appendix A.

Petitions

Petitions are prayer requests. Typically, a petition is a formal written request signed by people asking an authority to take a specific action. While it isn't necessary to put your prayer request in writing, it can be a cathartic part of journaling and contemplative thought. You will have equally effective results from reading and repeating the petition. The petitions listed with each of the everyday angels are provided to give you some ideas when you are ready to ask for help and guidance. Talk with your angels like you would talk to your best friend or a very close family member. Angels have the very specific duty of being the intermediaries between humans and the Divine. In order to perform their duties, they must be asked. Let yourself pray. Petition these Divine beings. Let the angels help you.

Affirmations

Affirmations are positive statements to aid you in shifting your thoughts toward your intended outcome or goal. Repeat the positive affirmations associated with a given everyday angel to amplify your focus on the positive changes. These thoughts will eliminate negative or self-sabotaging thoughts. Match the affirmation with the sparkling gemstone you've chosen to assist you. Bring the affirmation to mind when you inhale the essential oil. These affirmations are designed to assist you on all levels—mentally, emotionally, physically, and spiritually.

• • • • • •

All these tools—chakras, colors, gemstones, scents, supportive archangels, petitions, and affirmations—are your allies in maintaining your awareness on what you want in your life. When you are being mindful, you are conscious of having a thought, word, action, or emotion that signals the opposite of your goals. For example, wear turquoise or light blue when you want to invite the aid of the Angel of Communication or red when you want the Angel of Vitality and Energy to help you with endurance. The information in this book, combined with your intention, can help you align yourself on all levels to receive the angelic guidance you request. Look through the table of contents to find the most applicable topic or angel to help you through your current situation.

Angels respond to your thoughts and your petitions. Be clear on what you are creating. When you are conscious of anything that conflicts with your intentions, you can use your tools to remind yourself of your petition. Remember, the angels respond to your requests and take action on your behalf based on your thoughts, words, actions, and emotions, which are broadcasted through telepathy and vibration.

GUARDIAN ANGEL

*H*ow can I feel my Guardian Angel's presence? How can my Guardian Angel help me in various aspects of my life? Will my Guardian Angel protect me and keep me safe and sound?

Call on your Guardian Angel when you need help with any type of situation. Your Guardian Angel is an amalgamation of *all* the everyday angels mentioned in this book. This means your Guardian Angel is really many angels or a legion of angels at your beck and call. Your Guardian Angel has been by your side from the moment of your birth and will remain with you until the moment of your passing from the earthly realm. At that time, your Angel of Transition will take over to help you into your next reality. Your Guardian Angel's mission is to protect and guide you throughout your life. Remember to ask for this angel's assistance with specific requests. All you have to do is think with your Guardian Angel in mind and help will be on the way! Use the various prayers and petitions throughout this book as inspiration for wording your request. This angel of yours does it all!

Chakras

All seven chakras for the purpose of becoming fully awakened in this life's experience.

Colors

Iridescent white to help you get a sense of what your Guardian Angel "looks like." *Pastel blue* for ease in listening to and hearing messages from your Guardian Angel. *Pastel pink* to feel loved and supported.

Gemstones

Angelite for ease in communication and to remember to ask for help. *Blue lace agate* to hear and follow Divine guidance. *Celestite* to recognize and implement the symbols sent from the celestial realm and interpret those messages. *Chrysoprase* for feelings of comfort and support. *Kyanite* to maintain balanced alignment with the Divine. *Pink calcite* to feel the love of angels, saints, and God. *Rose quartz* to express the love that you are. *Scolecite* to recognize the vibrations of the angelic realm in your vicinity. *Selenite* for physical alignment with angels and spirit guides. *Tabular clear quartz*, known as a telepathic communication aid, to send and receive pictures, thoughts, and feelings from the angels.

Essential Oils

Benzoin resin for stability and to improve mood and strengthen the protective field surrounding you. *Lavender* to elicit feelings of comfort and well-being. *Mandarin* for connection with the sweetness of life. *Pink grapefruit* to encourage heart-centered focus and clarity. *Orange* to raise your vibrations to high levels of joy and laughter. *Vanilla* to encourage feelings of calm, safety, and peace.

Supportive Archangels

Archangel Gabriel for inspired guidance. *Archangel Michael* for constant protection. *Archangel Raphael* for healing and good health. *Archangel Uriel* for universal flow.

Suggested Petition

Oh, Guardian Angel, please come and help me. I don't know what to do or how to do it. Guide and inspire me! Bring me Divine insight and inspiration. Please light my path and send supportive people into my life. Thank you!

You can also use this traditional prayer: "Angel of God, my guardian dear, to whom God's love commits you here. Ever this day be at my side to light and guard, to rule and guide."

Affirmations

I know I always have an angel at my side. I am grateful that angels light my path and inspire me. I am able to handle any situation that arises. I appreciate the support available to me in all areas of my life.

ANGEL OF ABUNDANCE
AND PROSPERITY

*W*here do I feel lack? Do I have plenty of food, water, and financial stability? Are there helpful people in my life?

Call on the Angel of Abundance and Prosperity when you perceive a deficiency in some aspect of your life. Take time to uncover how and why you feel like you don't have enough or that there isn't plenty for you and those around you. Be as specific as possible. Once you've identified the lack, call on the Angel of Abundance and Prosperity to help you see how you can improve the situation. Remember to ask for the motivation to take action to change your reality—or your perception of reality. Partner this angel with the Angel of Gratitude to amplify the awareness that you actually do have plenty of everything you will ever need and to increase your ability to share your abundance. Simply recognize your good fortune. Focus on your vast abundance and you will attract more.

Chakras

Heart chakra to give and receive while focused on gratitude. *Root chakra* to feel secure in knowing that all you ever need is available to you. *Solar plexus chakra* to activate the confidence and courage to be prosperous and enjoy abundance. *Third eye chakra* to think clearly and use your intuition and intelligence to manage your prosperity.

Colors

Copper to be a conduit of plenty for all. *Gold* to increase financial flow and higher wisdom. *Green* to be proficient and skillful in financial matters. *Silver* to always find and use the benefits of the silver lining (the good in situations that, on the surface, appear negative).

Gemstones

Amethyst to release negative beliefs regarding material wealth. *Carnelian* to have the courage and motivation to take action to manifest the abundance you desire. *Clear quartz* to gain clarity and realization; use them to amplify the abundance in your life. *Copper* to activate the part of you that channels plenty for yourself and everyone around you. *Emerald* to recognize and be grateful for abundance and to amplify love. *Green aventurine* to realize your good fortune. *Green tourmaline* to see and feel love, luck, wealth, and success. *Pyrite* to recognize golden opportunities and welcome them into your life. *Sapphire* to improve wisdom, loyalty, and authenticity in all dealings involving money.

Essential Oils

Basil to awaken your connection with your guides and angels and remember spiritual abundance. *Bergamot* to improve mental clarity, focus, and self-confidence and to activate connection with the angelic realm. *Cinnamon* to attract prosperity, increase confidence, remove blocks, and activate your mind to achieve new results. *Patchouli* to attract love and money.

Supportive Archangels

Archangel Ariel to motivate you to take the action necessary to increase your wealth. *Archangel Barachiel*, God's blessings, for good fortune and to help open your heart to receive abundance. *Archangel Chamuel* to boost your self-confidence and become more successful in your career. *Archangel Jophiel* for an abundance of beauty and wisdom. *Archangel Metatron* to motivate you to take positive action to create prosperity. *Archangel Sachiel* to increase success and material gain. *Archangel Uriel* to imbue you with a vibe of creative action, prosperity, and wisdom.

Suggested Petition

Oh, Angel of Abundance and Prosperity! I am calling on you today to help me with my needs. Please support me in surrounding myself with good friends and family members. I ask that you assist me with my basic requirements of food, shelter, and water but also with my greater needs, including business, finances, and downtime. I want to laugh often and live fully, so please help me to know how. Guide me to see and sense the way to achieve abundance and prosperity in all areas of my life. Thank you!

Affirmations

I am grateful for the abundance and prosperity in my life. I enjoy my loyal and supportive friends and family. Everything I need or want is always available to me. Love, wealth, and plenitude come naturally to me. I have many blessings. I have plenty of money and plenty to share. Blessings are constantly flowing into my life.

ANGEL OF ACTION

*W*hat do I need to accomplish? Have I been procrastinating and if so, why? What do I need to know or do to start moving toward my goals?

Call on the Angel of Action when you feel stymied and frustrated with your progress, either generally in your life or with regard to a specific project. Whether you are feeling a perceived block or certain situations are obstructing your ability to move forward, call on the Angel of Action to help get things flowing and motivate you to take a step—any step—toward your intended goal. Gain clarity on the reason you feel the way you do, refocus your attention and your imagination on the goal or completion, and request that the Angel of Action lead you to the information or resources you need to take action. A bit of extra confidence and self-esteem can go a long way, so ask this angel to help you see and remember your inherent ability to move forward.

Chakras

Navel chakra to activate creative solutions to manifest your intentions. *Root chakra* to feel energized, grounded, safe, and motivated. *Solar plexus chakra* for the confidence, courage, and clarity to make progress.

Colors

Orange for the courage to move forward and manifest desired results. *Red* for passionate action. *Yellow* to activate inner strength and self-confidence.

Gemstones

Carnelian to invoke the key phrase *manifesto presto,* meaning immediate action and manifestation. *Citrine* for self-confidence and courage. *Fire agate* to light a proverbial fire under you to get motivated and make things happen. *Garnet* to activate your vitality and vigor to accomplish great things. *Golden topaz* to have the courage to step forward with joy and enthusiasm. *Orange calcite* to help you integrate the changes in your way of life after you've taken action. *Ruby* to energize your passion for life and increase vibrancy and productivity. *Sunstone* to have the confidence to shine light on your path so you can find the way to take action.

Essential Oils

Allspice to align with action-oriented masculine energy. *Black pepper* to amplify confidence and the ability to move forward with purpose. *Cardamom* to stimulate action and for the ability to integrate everything going on around you for clear awareness of how to move forward. *Cinnamon* to activate the imagination, which is key to visualizing your future and therefore creating ease as you take action. *Lemon* to move forward with clarity and confidence even in the face of setbacks. *Peppermint* to access past experiences as valuable lessons, which allows you to propel forward with ease. *Rosemary* to increase mental acuity, thereby allowing for greater productivity.

Supportive Archangels

Archangel Ariel for vitality and vigor. *Archangel Camael* to align with movement and improved energy levels. *Archangel Melchizedek* to keep you grounded and safe. *Archangel Uriel* for creative action.

Suggested Petition

Oh, Angel of Action! Please come here now to help me move forward and take action on something I need to accomplish. Help me see myself more clearly and understand what is preventing me from starting and/or completing the task or deed. This achievement may be a piece of the puzzle I need to live my life's purpose. Help me take the necessary steps at this time in my life. Thank you!

Affirmations

I effortlessly visualize my goals and aspirations. My imagination is the key to my success. My ideas are fresh and creative. I take action to manifest my artistic thoughts. I step forward in life with confidence and purpose. I am grateful that my vital life force provides me with the energy and motivation to live life to the fullest!

ANGEL OF ANGER MANAGEMENT

*W*hy am I angry? Who is aggravating me? How can I use this passionate emotion to realign the situation?

Call on the Angel of Anger Management when you need to control your rage and disappointment in order to use the challenge at hand to improve a situation. Ask for assistance with patience and diplomacy so that you can use the realizations arising from your anger to make positive changes for you and those around you. Remember that there is nothing wrong with passionately establishing clear boundaries. Often, vehemence restores equilibrium and creates future opportunities to use sage wisdom. Understanding a situation from a place of experience is a powerful tool. Take the time to look at yourself and your interactions to see if your anger is misdirected toward people, places, or situations that have nothing to do with your reason for being angry. Call on this angel to help you rectify this behavior immediately for the good of all concerned. This angel can aid in releasing fear that is often associated with anger and setting up a field of protection and safety.

Chakras

Crown chakra for clarity and understanding. *Heart chakra* to awaken loving feelings in order to dissolve anger. *Root chakra* to understand the foundation and source of your anger.

Colors

Black to remove negative energy and activate protection. *Blue* to calm savage energy and eliminate hysterical reactions. *Brown* to ground and soften the magnitude of how anger is expressed without removing it for self-examination. *Green* to heal the issue. *Metallic gray* to deflect negative outside influences from intruding and prevent others from fueling the anger. *Red*, the color of anger, to get to the source or origin of the anger.

Gemstones

Black tourmaline to stay grounded and calm while deflecting negative thoughts and emotions. *Chrysocolla* to bring about peace, calm, and understanding. *Garnet* to get the negative vibes out of your system while using exercise or other action-oriented activities such as drumming or primal screaming. *Green opal* to heal the source of the angst while reducing inflamed emotions. *Jet*, a fossilized charcoal, to clean and clear the uncomfortable vibes of anger. *Lapis lazuli* to attract peace and encourage spending time in inner reflection. *Rose quartz* for increasing feelings of love, safety, and comfort. *Ruby* to productively utilize the anger as a source for learning and as a catalyst for personal growth. *Sapphire* to bring about deeper understanding and a clear view of the truth. *Smoky quartz* to refocus your efforts away from distractions as you release your emotional baggage. *Sodalite* to be at peace with yourself and the world around you.

Essential Oils

Angelica to realize subconscious fears and awaken higher understanding. *Benzoin* to heal the anger and bring a sense of calm and peace. *Chamomile* for composure, inner peace, and patience. *Frankincense* to encourage deep breaths and bring forth compassion for self and others. *Lavender* to heal and calm, relax and release, and renew and restore balance. *Orange* to calm the nerves and restore focus on joy and confidence. *Sweet marjoram* to release repetitive and/or negative thoughts associated with fears, phobias, and obsessions. *Vetiver* to rebalance raw emotions, feelings, and out-of-control responses. *Ylang-ylang* to calm erratic emotions.

Supportive Archangels

Archangel Chamuel to open your heart center and activate loving vibrations and peaceful relations. *Archangel Michael* to remove fears, phobias, and obsessions. *Archangel Muriel* to bring peace and harmony through emotional balance. *Archangel Sabrael* to release jealousy and negative energy. *Archangel Uriel* to transform painful memories and instill tranquility.

Suggested Petition

Oh, Angel of Anger Management! I am feeling resentful and full of rage. Please help me calm down and release these uncomfortable emotions. Help me take steps to resolve feelings of bitterness and jealousy and recover from this struggle. Help me release repetitive thoughts about anger-provoking issues and be free of this tense vibe. Please help people who direct their anger toward me find a way to communicate with kindness. Thank you!

Affirmations

All is well. I am calm, relaxed, and at peace. I know that intense feelings of anger will pass. I release resentment and frustration and open myself up to healing energy. It is easy for me to stay calm. I let go of what is no longer for my highest good and go with the flow in a calm, peaceful manner.

ANGEL OF ANIMAL COMPANIONS

*H*ow can I be a better companion to the animals in my surroundings? Do my animal friends need something more from me to have a better life? Can I hear or intuit what the animals around me want or need?

The Angel of Animal Companions helps make you a better human companion to animals by activating your telepathic abilities: mind-to-mind and heart-to-heart communication. Call on this angel to help you look deeply into yourself to check in on your own level of authenticity, dependability, and fidelity so that you can build strong, healthy relationships with your animal companions. This angel can help you consciously dedicate time and attention to your furry, feathered, and/or scaly friends. Open your heart to enjoy the benefits of connecting with the animals in your life and notice how your overall well-being improves. Let this angel be your ally to open a bridge from your heart and mind to the heart and mind of animals and all Mother Nature's creatures. Improve your connection with the planet and remember that you are a steward and caregiver of all creatures everywhere.

Chakras

Crown chakra to align with the Divine spirit in all creatures great and small. *Heart chakra* to maintain a focus on loving kindness and compassionate action. *Root chakra* to help you stay focused on earth-centered connections with nature and all life. *Third eye chakra* to clearly see that all life matters and is interconnected. *Throat chakra* to communicate—listen well and express—with all life.

Colors

Black to be a protector for all animals, including insects, reptiles, bird, sea life, and beyond. *Blue* to maintain a sense of calm reverence and a peaceful attitude when interacting with animals. *Brown* to stay focused on the creatures of this planet in a supportive role. *Red* to take passionate action to be a guardian to all nature. *Turquoise* to communicate and understand interspecies communication.

Gemstones

Cobra jasper, composed of fossilized snail shells and palm, to strengthen your connection with the animal kingdom. *Larimar* to align you with interspecies communication to hear and know messages from animals. *Rainforest jasper* to increase your connection to plants, trees, and animals. *Tabular quartz* to aid you in visualizing and imagining your message through mental images from heart-to-heart and mind-to-mind communications with animals and humans. *Tree agate* to increase mutual understanding between yourself and animals, including your pets as well as those that live in nature. *Turquoise* to listen well and to hear, know, and speak the truth.

Essential Oils

Amber to align your consciousness with the natural world and amplify nature's vast communication network. *Cypress* to heighten consciousness and improve your understanding of and connection with the animal kingdom and all of nature. *Patchouli* to widen your perspective and enhance your ability to look at things from different angles, thereby becoming more aware of the spirits of animals and nature. *Petitgrain* to release mental obstacles and increase clarity, thereby enhancing your potential to receive communication from animals. *Pine* to remind you that you are responsible for the well-being of all animals. *Vetiver* for earth-centered spiritual pursuits, earth-based rituals, and shamanic journeywork to increase your ability to commune with animals.

Supportive Archangels

Archangel Ariel, the patron of animals, to protect the earth's environment and its many animal inhabitants. *Archangel Haniel* to improve your communication skills with animals and the rest of nature. *Archangel Raphael* for overall health and the well-being of animals and humans alike. *Archangel Thuriel* for interspecies connection, especially human and animal communication. *Archangel Uriel* to embrace planetary citizenship and stewardship.

Suggested Petition

Oh, Angel of Animal Companions! I am in search of a deeper spiritual connection with all animals, especially the animals who are part of my family. Help me hear and listen to my animal companions. Let their messages be received by me and integrated so that we all have a fulfilling, loving relationship. Remind me to spend time in nature. Guide me when I am outdoors and open my consciousness to commune with the wildlife. Inspire and motivate me to take action to support a better life for all animals on our planet in any way possible. Thank you!

Affirmations

I communicate from my heart to the hearts of others, human and animal alike. I visualize and send mental pictures as I verbally express myself. I am blessed with wonderful animal companions and great friends. I open my consciousness to various forms of expression and express myself with ease and grace. I have an intimate connection with Mother Nature, including all animal life.

ANGEL OF AWAKENING

*H*ave I been asleep and need to awaken? What am I awakening from? How will awakening help me in my daily life?

The Angel of Awakening is your guide to being a conscientious member of your family, your workplace, and society. Being awakened brings with it the responsibility of acting from your highest morals and always dealing with others in an honest, ethical manner. When you decide you want to wake up from unconscious rote behavior, your life will unfold to help you meet this goal. Spiritual awakening is the key to remembering and living your life's purpose. Use this angel as a guide to help you understand how to awaken on all levels—spiritually, mentally, emotionally, and physically. Ask the Angel of Awakening to improve your situational awareness, the awareness of the elements in your space, and what is happening around you. Let this angel shine light on your experiences to improve your ability to discern various energies around you—to know which energies are yours and which belong to others.

Chakras

Crown chakra to connect with your unlimited potential and intuition, and to increase the possibility of self-realization. *Heart chakra* to access the bridge between the lower three chakras and the upper three chakras with compassion, love, and understanding. *Third eye chakra* to awaken your consciousness and access the records of all that is, all that was, and all potential future realities. *Throat chakra* to connect with Divine timing, angels, and invisible beings of light to help guide you on your spiritual path to awakening.

Colors

Iridescent white to shine light on your path of awakening. *Navy blue* to deepen your meditation practice. *Purple* to transform challenges and tap into intuitive abilities.

Gemstones

Apophyllite to magnify the meditation experience for a deeper, clearer, more profound practice. *Aquamarine* to joyfully awaken spiritually and for self-development work. *Citrine* to become conscious of the repetitive patterns of self-limiting thoughts. *Clear quartz* to increase perspective and visions that bring awareness and understanding of life situations. *Dolomite* to objectively observe your behaviors and issues to make a shift toward more enlightened behaviors and actions. *Herkimer diamond* to improve spiritual sight and heighten your consciousness and awareness. *Kyanite* to connect with higher realms of consciousness. *Selenite* to connect with higher wisdom and knowledge as well as with Divine wisdom, spirit guides, and angels.

Essential Oils

Basil to remember spiritual abundance, awaken your connection with guides and angels, and remember past lives for the purpose of your soul's evolution. *Cypress* to awaken a deeper understanding of your ancestors and improve your ability to commune with your loved ones on the Other Side. *Frankincense* to enhance your meditation practice, align with higher realms of consciousness, and improve your ability to recognize spiritual and mystical experiences. *Grapefruit* for its mind-clearing properties and to help you raise your consciousness to receive messages from the angelic realm. *Peppermint* to wake you up both physically and spiritually so that you can remain present during your meditation practice.

Supportive Archangels

Archangel Chamuel to release fear, increase the courage to rise above life challenges, and use the experience to awaken your awareness to see the bigger picture. *Archangel Gabriel* to open your spiritual ears to hear messages and guidance. *Archangel Metatron* to align with higher states of consciousness. *Archangel Uriel* for spiritual and intellectual enlightenment and wisdom. *Archangel Zaphkiel* for greater understanding and mindfulness.

Suggested Petition

Oh, Angel of Awakening! Please come here now to help me find the answers within. Let me become aware of the wisdom of the ancestors and align myself with higher consciousness. Show me how to be mindful and present at all times. Let me always find the light within the darkness. Bring me clarity and understanding. Help me bring forth the courage to empower myself and others to reach enlightenment. Instill in me the grace of understanding and let me be merciful. Thank you!

Affirmations

The Divine spark resides within me. I get great ideas all the time and act on them. I easily tap into universal wisdom. I am one with the knowledge of my ancestors. I easily clear away energetic cobwebs and open portals of awareness to increase insights and higher knowledge.

ANGEL OF BALANCED EMOTIONS

*W*hy do I feel like my emotions are out of control? What thoughts are fueling the emotions I am experiencing? How can I release beliefs that are no longer true or applicable?

The Angel of Balanced Emotions is your guide to detach from drama and instead cultivate tools to develop inner strength. This angel shines light on your path to know your own essence. With this knowing in place, you are able to align with peace and love and release the need to feel like you must enable yourself or another. Enabling someone encourages the out-of-balance emotions, either directly or indirectly. Call on this angel when you need to let go of neediness and increase healthy detachment from people, places, and situations. This angelic helper is also a perfect ally to quell emotional outbursts. With objective observation and situational awareness as tools to maintain balance, you are able to let go and let others live their lives and attract loyal friends who let you live your life.

Chakras

Navel chakra to increase the courage to be who you are and stand strong in your personal power. *Solar plexus chakra* for high self-esteem and the ability to process and integrate all that is needed to balance feelings. *Third eye chakra* to have a clear view of the truth and to see your life experiences from a higher perspective.

Colors

Olive green to aid in the integration and digestion of life. *Pastel blue* to feel peace. *Peach* to open up to a deeper understanding through the vibration of love. *Seafoam green* to experience nurturing energy and the support of loving friends and family. *Yellow* to integrate and process situations so you can be peaceful.

Gemstones

Blue topaz to increase your awareness of what you are feeling and help calm your emotions. *Black tourmaline* to draw out negative emotions and release uncontrollable reactivity. *Lepidolite with pink tourmaline inclusions* to balance emotions and mood swings with compassion and mercy for yourself and others. *Peridot* to release feeling of jealousy. *Prasiolite* to accept your emotions and emotional challenges through acceptance and compassion. *Prehnite* to help you deal with feelings of unrest during times of change and uncertain conditions. *Stilbite*, a member of the zeolite family of minerals, to calm your emotions and shift your perceptions to allow for objectivity. *Sugilite* to transform disturbing emotions or ignorant beliefs, especially as they relate to your perceptions of others. *Sunstone* to help evaporate watery, out-of-balance emotions and lift you toward optimism. *Tiger's eye* to release feelings of jealousy and aid in mastering emotions during periods of upheaval. *Unakite* to help align your mind with your heart when dealing with emotional imbalances.

Essential Oils

Chamomile to release stress and experience tranquility. *Clary sage* to help you live and let live. *Elemi* to calm and reduce emotional outbursts. *Geranium* to encourage hormonal balance and induce a sense of peace. *Juniper* to detoxify your mind of repetitive negative thought patterns. *Lavender* to invoke inner peace and calm and soothe rampant emotions. *Sweet marjoram* to calm paranoid thoughts and reduce feelings of hysteria.

Supportive Archangels

Archangel Michael to support you during emotional challenges and protect you from outside influences when you are most vulnerable. *Archangel Muriel* for inner peace and tranquility. *Archangel Raphael* for emotional healing. *Archangel Sabrael* to heal jealousy or envy that stems from you or from outside of you.

Suggested Petition

Oh, Angel of Balanced Emotions! I need help finding my center and calming down. Please help me feel at peace so that I can stop crying, yelling, or ranting. I want to be still and release the need to act out. I want to feel serene and let go of any hysteria. Help me invoke a vibe of inner peace to soothe my rampant emotions and detox from negative thought patterns. Help me cultivate a greater understanding of myself and others to increase my happiness and self-confidence. Thank you!

Affirmations

I embrace all of my emotions as I allow balance to return to my life. Nurturing energy surrounds me, bringing my emotional body back into alignment. I attract inner peace and great joy every day in many ways. I am blessed with a deep understanding of my feelings. I move about my life with poise and grace.

ANGEL OF BLESSINGS

*W*hy do I feel that I need more blessings? What part of my daily life feels lacking in some way? How can I put my attention on all that is good in my life?

The Angel of Blessings supports your efforts to keep your attention on the many ways you do feel lucky and happy. This is the angel who helps you recognize the many good things in your life, and you feel blessed. As you realize that you have all the help you need to lighten your potential burdens, you will align even more with the good things in your daily experiences. Practice gratitude in all that you do. Think of all the ways you are grateful. Include people and places in your thoughts of gratitude and send blessings their way. Use the Angel of Blessings to dedicate your life in Divine service to be a blessing for all beings. Call on this angel to help you remember that good fortune and blessings are often the result of years of good thoughts, good deeds, hard work, and an open heart.

Chakras

All chakras to be open to receiving blessings on every level.

Colors

Copper to be a conduit that supplies blessings for others as well as yourself. *Gold* to shine a bright light on the amazing magnitude of blessings that exist in your life. *Orange* for the ability, courage, and motivation to easily manifest anything you need. *Silver* to link your innate receptive awareness with your intuitive nature and to see the positive in all situations. *White* for clarity and to have a clear view of your unlimited potential.

Gemstones

Diamond to turn up the light of your spiritual nature and to strengthen your inner foundations of knowledge and wisdom. *Epidote* to feel grateful for current blessings as well as all the blessings still to come. *Green aventurine* to embrace that you are incredibly lucky and blessed and to open yourself to draw in even more blessings. *Green goldstone* to be consciously available to receive blessings and prosperity in your life. *Herkimer diamond* to illuminate your true nature of love and kindness and to activate mental clarity. *Jade* to align with good fortune and the awareness that you deserve good fortune. *Kunzite* to know how blessed you are and to spread blessings wherever you go and wherever you are. *Rose quartz* to amplify love and to attract all that is good. *Tiger's eye* to dissipate and deflect jealousy from yourself or others.

Essential Oils

Geranium to attract blessings in the form of friendship and good relationships. *Grapefruit* to open your heart to receive blessings, joy, and happiness and to evoke feelings of bliss and comfort. *Jasmine* for remembering that you are blessed with nurturing vibrations wherever you are. *Lavender* to allow blessings to come and to fully experience the sweetness of love. *Lemongrass* to feel the blessings of self-confidence and courage.

Supportive Archangels

Archangel Ariel for general health and vitality. *Archangel Gabriel* to improve your understanding and recognition of your blessings. *Archangel Jophiel* for inner wisdom and to notice the beauty all around you. *Archangel Raziel* to embrace and use your spiritual gifts. *Archangel Uriel* to be blessed with wisdom and spiritual enlightenment.

Suggested Petition

Oh, Angel of Blessings! Please help me increase my mental capacity to integrate love, abundance, good health, financial stability, and unconditional love into my life. Help me focus on the many blessings I experience daily and relax into the knowledge that nothing is lacking. Thank you in advance for assuring good health, abundant wealth, and the ability to give and receive love fully and completely. Thank you!

Affirmations

All that I need is available to me. I am happy for other people's good fortune and blessings. I have an open heart. I am grateful for all the blessings still to come. All that surrounds me and all that is attracted to me is love. I draw love, joy, and happiness into my life, and I am comforted. Blessings are always present.

ANGEL OF CAREER

*A*m I a natural at organizing and managing others, either at home or at the office? Do I focus on the long-term goals and take action to meet them? Do I have business acumen and determination?

Call on the Angel of Career to gain a clear understanding of your business or your life purpose with regard to your career. This angel can help you be a visionary and allow for the unimpeded flow of information, ideas, and realizations to create or grow a successful business. Ask this angel to help you make a list of what it will take to accomplish your goals. Imagine the Angel of Career to motivate you to take the actions required. It requires courage and confidence to create your business and to take action to fulfill your vision. With this angel's assistance, uncover your business acumen, tap into your determination, and access your willingness to make unlimited income doing what you love to do. This angel encourages you to be adventurous and farsighted as you think outside the box to implement your ideas into action regarding your professional pursuits.

Chakras

Navel chakra to activate your creativity and courageously move forward. *Root chakra* for focus on the core needs of the business, including staffing, payroll, and sufficient funds. *Solar plexus chakra* for the self-confidence and mental clarity to achieve your dreams and goals. *Third eye chakra* for intelligence, organization, and visionary action to create or grow your business. *Throat chakra* to communicate well with staff members and business associates.

Colors

Blue for peaceful interactions. *Green* for prosperity, abundance, and good money skills. *Orange* to creatively visualize ideas and bring them into reality. *Yellow* for mental clarity and confidence.

Gemstones

Andalusite to encourage earth-centered focus to assure that all the basic needs of your business are in place. *Bismuth* to aid in creating pathways for the development of creative ideas. *Citrine*, known as the merchant's stone, to have clarity and confidence to make your business all that it can be. *Green aventurine* to imbue the energy of prosperity, abundance, and financial success. *Moldavite* to allow far-out concepts to flow through you, enabling you to be a visionary in your field.

Essential Oils

Basil to increase your moneymaking and entrepreneurial abilities. *Black pepper* to speed up your thought processes, relieve sluggishness, enhance memory, and help with mental acuity regarding business transactions. *Cinnamon* to increase your capacity to earn money. *Clove* to visualize and manifest your business ideas while deflecting jealousy and ill will. *Mandarin* to enhance mental clarity and a sharp mind. *Patchouli* for grounding and to release laziness through focus and action. *Rosemary* to deflect jealousy and to improve memory and mental alertness.

Supportive Archangels

Archangel Gabriel to improve connection with inspired thoughts and application to entrepreneurial activities. *Archangel Metatron* to take action on the awareness of your soul's purpose. *Archangel Michael* for intelligence, observation, and perspective. *Archangel Raziel* to embrace your gifts of intuition and prophecy as it relates to being the visionary for your business. *Archangel Sabrael* to ward off jealousy and protect your business ideas and property.

Suggested Petition

Oh, Angel of Career! Please partner with me as I operate my business. Guide me and watch over me as I make financial decisions and take the risks necessary to make a difference. Help me to be confidently in charge as I organize and manage my business. Show me the way as I hire employees so that I find the right people to fulfill the vision of my work. Help me as I develop and launch new products and services. Let me be an innovator and make a difference in people's lives with the work that I do. Thank you!

Affirmations

Prosperity abounds in my life, and goodness multiplies through my entrepreneurial efforts. Many people with plenty of resources need the services I offer, and I am happy to be of service. I'm self-motivated and productive. I complete my tasks and creative projects with ease. I am grateful for all my creative and business skills. I earn unlimited income doing what I love.

ANGEL OF CHANGE

*W*hat's changing in my life? How will these changes affect my future? Why am I feeling apprehensive about these new life experiences?

The Angel of Change is an angel that is always helping you shift and flow with change, because, after all, the only constant in life is change. Call on the Angel of Change during transitional times, like ending or starting a new relationship, moving to a new residence, becoming an empty nester, or experiencing menopause. This angel will awaken your awareness and enable you to realize if you keep making the same mistakes over and over again and how to heal the source of such issues. With this angel on your team, you can recognize that life flows in circles and all cycles shift and change. Let this angel help you focus on how you want your reality to manifest in alignment with the changes that are occurring. Remember that your thoughts and beliefs create reality and that you are in charge of your own world. The Angel of Change supports you so that you can stop worrying and have the faith and courage you need to navigate life's twists and turns.

Chakras

Navel chakra to creatively approach changing situations. *Root chakra* to be firmly grounded, balanced, and supported at all times. *Solar plexus chakra* for the confidence needed to deal with change.

Colors

Black to know that all that you need is found within the inner recesses of your consciousness. *Gold* to develop your intuitive senses and increase your ability to bring forth inspired self-awareness, which brings comfort during change. *Magenta* to grasp conflicting feelings and emotions to bring them into balance with intentional loving kindness. *Swirly, iridescent purple* to whisk away the old so that new joyful experiences can unfold. *White* to invoke the power of foresight and the light of prophecy.

Gemstones

Amethyst to avoid harmful distractions and to change old habits through conscious intent. *Dolomite* to create new pathways of consciousness by opening up to unexplored avenues for raising your awareness. *Indigo gabbro*, also known as *merlinite*, to shift and alchemize any situation. *Lepidolite*, a silicate-containing lithium, to help you foster a reasonable hold on reality, open neural pathways in your brain, and encourage a detached outlook on situations. *Optical calcite* to increase the ability to see information clearly in order to "see through" situations, thereby amplifying the self-confidence you need to navigate change. *Orange calcite* to activate a creative approach to situations that are initially challenging. *Pietersite* to strengthen confidence in your perceptions to see clearly through illusions as life shifts. *Pink calcite* to embrace kindheartedness as you go through life-changing situations. *Stromatolite*, among the oldest fossils on Earth, to dislodge negative thoughts and to gain information about the causes of repetitive patterns to create positive change.

Essential Oils

Basil to help you see that you are the one directing the creation and perception of your personal reality. *Elemi* to encourage you to make the changes needed to restructure unhelpful thoughts rotating in your consciousness. *Lemongrass* for clearing your mind and to help you process all that is going on. *Petitgrain* to increase self-confidence in relation to life changes.

Supportive Archangels

Archangel Gabriel to receive inspiration and guidance while going through changes. *Archangel Uriel* for spiritual enlightenment and peace. *Archangel Zadkiel* for ease in the transformation process. *Guardian Angel* to feel guided and safe as you navigate the changing landscape of your life.

Suggested Petition

Oh, Angel of Change! Please help me relax and flow with the ever-turning cycles that create change. Help me find ways to consciously effectuate change with the foresight to understand why things are changing. Inspire me with ideas so that I can see and experience the blessings within this change and understand how this change will ultimately make my life better. I want to know and remember that everything happens for a reason. Help me easily adapt and make the necessary adjustments so that my new way of life is happy and fulfilling. Thank you!

Affirmations

I create my reality. I know how to make positive changes to transform my life in a desired way. It's easy for me to transmute challenging situations into beneficial ones. I easily adjust my attitude to create a happier me. I embrace the sunshine as well as the rain, and I am in balance with all life. I embrace change with ease and grace.

ANGEL OF CHILDBIRTH

*A*m I ready to have a child? Have I prepared myself mentally, emotionally, physically, and spiritually to be a parent? Am I financially stable and able to support this child?

Call on the Angel of Childbirth to support your decision to bring a new life into the word. Ask the angel to ensure that your reproductive system and mammary glands are in tip-top shape. This angel supports both parents from the time they conceive their baby through childbirth. Parenting begins before conception so ask this angel to aid in the mental, emotional, and spiritual processes that you will go through in preparation for becoming a parent. Invite this angel into your life during the early stages of planning a family so that you are fertile in body, mind, and spirit and have positive thoughts and emotions while preparing for conscious conception, throughout pregnancy, and during birth. Ask this angel to help you to trust this process and all the changes that the birth of your child will bring into your life. This angel is your ally to support you if you are unable to conceive. Call on the Angel of Childbirth to ease your grief and to show you ways you can embrace alternative avenues for parenthood. This angel can be of great assistance to open you up to other ways you can use your nurturing energy, even if parenthood isn't part of your path.

Chakras

Crown chakra to align with the spirit of your child. *Heart chakra* to amplify love and blessings. *Navel chakra* for ease during the birth process. *Root chakra* to feel safe and sound at all times. *Throat chakra* to communicate with your child beyond words.

Colors

Blue for deep inner peace and higher wisdom. *Red* to connect with general health and vitality.

Gemstones

Aquamarine for support if you are planning a water birth for your baby. *Bloodstone* for a healthy pregnancy and ease in delivery. *Carnelian* to bring processes into motion with courage and creative visualization. *Cobra jasper* to support fertility, pregnancy, and the birthing process. *Fire agate* to increase endurance and ease the birthing process. *Garnet* to increase the energy levels needed to birth a child and all that follows in the years to come. *Hematite* to maintain a sense of calm and inner peace. *Orange calcite* for a fertile life and ease in bringing a baby into the world. *Ruby* to amplify strength, vitality, and lifelong endurance as a parent.

Essential Oils

During pregnancy, use these essential oils with caution and only under the guidance of a well-educated aromatherapy doula or medical professional.

Clary sage to relax and find comfort. *Fennel* to stimulate uterine contractions and lactation under the guidance of a professional. *Geranium* to regulate glandular functions and hormones. *Jasmine* to reduce stress and stimulate uterine contractions. *Sage* to reduce stress and regulate blood pressure and increase feelings of euphoria. *Sweet marjoram* to aid in dilation and reduce blood pressure. *Ylang-ylang* to calm, relax, and reduce pain.

Supportive Archangels

Archangel Auriel to align with the Divine Feminine. *Archangel Avartiel* to ward off miscarriages and protect both men and women during pregnancy. *Archangel Zadkiel* to support the birth of a healthy child. *Archangel Zuriel* for protection of the mother-to-be and to provide comfort during childbirth.

Suggested Petition

Oh, Angel of Childbirth! Please lend your support for the birthing process so that my baby easily travels through the birth canal and enters this world safely. Keep my baby healthy and ease any discomfort for us during this process. Please watch over my partner so that he/she can be a supportive co-parent, now and in the future. I request that my hormones become rebalanced and that my mental and emotional states are healthy and aligned with the greatest good. Thank you!

Affirmations

I am excited to become a parent. My energy flows perfectly. My blood is full of life-giving oxygen, and it circulates through my system just as it should for good health. My physical structure is strong. The baby is growing perfectly within and all is well. We are blessed to be parents to this child. The time is now!

ANGEL OF COMFORT

*W*hy do I need comforting? How can I make myself feel more comfortable? How can I best deal with the emotions I am currently experiencing?

Call on the Angel of Comfort when you realize or perceive that you don't have anyone but yourself to support you during a time of personal suffering. Turn to this angel when you feel inconsolable. Imagine you are telling this angel all that is on your mind and in your heart. Pour out your suffering and let yourself feel comfort in return. Ask this angel to inspire you with ideas for comforting yourself to find the freedom you need. Pause and breathe deeply, visualize peaceful images, listen to soothing music, and practice gratitude. The practice of gratitude is a perfect tool to help you shift your attention away from painful emotions to recognize the blessings in your life, which will bring you comfort. Let the Angel of Comfort be your ally to show you the way to be free from distress, fear, and pain.

Chakras

Heart chakra to open your heart to feel love and kindness enveloping you. *Root chakra* to assure you that all is well and everything will be alright. *Solar plexus chakra* to help you access your inner power and source of peace.

Colors

Forest green to elicit feelings of being supported by the life-giving energies of all plant life. *Light blue* to feel inner peace and calm. *Metallic gray* to envelop you with a layer of protection. *Pastel pink* to experience being wrapped in supportive and loving matriarchal energy. *Seafoam green* to embrace and support the emotions you are experiencing.

Gemstones

Celestite to instill a sense of peace and comfort during tumultuous emotional times. *Chrysoprase* to bring forth a sense of being cared for, loved, and appreciated. *Dolomite* to find a way to comfort yourself when you are out of sorts. *Kunzite* to radiate love and receive loving vibrations that comfort you. *Pink calcite* to align with the Divine Mother for unconditional love and support. *Rose quartz* for situations when you need to feel comforted and surrounded by unconditional love. *Ruby in zoisite* to amplify the vibration of love, blessings, and comfort in all situations.

Essential Oils

Allspice to provide a sensation of warmth and relaxation during times of emotional stress. *Benzoin* to increase the mystical connection beyond conscious awareness to encourage transformation on a soul level. *Clary sage* to calm nervous energy, release stress, ground feelings and emotions, and bring about a sense of serenity. *Lavender* to clear and calm the mind, comfort your heart, and soothe and calm chaotic and rampant emotions.

Supportive Archangels

Archangel Chamuel to encourage friends to be at your side when you need support. *Archangel Michael* to bring forth feelings of comfort and safety. *Archangel Raphael* for healing any type of discomfort. *Archangel Zadkiel* to gain mental clarity and focused thinking, and to develop a logical approach to overcome uncomfortable situations.

Suggested Petition

Oh, Angel of Comfort! Please console me and remind me how to connect with the Divine. Let me feel the energy of the Divine Mother and imagine that she is rocking me in her arms as I release emotions and feelings that are causing me discomfort and grief. Help me accept my feelings as they are without judgment and also to let go of low feelings. Show me how to focus on the blessings in my life and be grateful for all that is good. Thank you!

Affirmations

I feel at ease. My friends and family are supportive and encouraging. Everything I need or want is always available to me. I am comforted and allow balance to return to my life. Uplifting vibes are available to me always. Nurturing energy surrounds me, bringing my emotional body into alignment. I attract inner peace and comfort every day in many ways.

ANGEL OF COMMUNICATION

*W*hat do I need to say and what do I need to hear? Am I being heard? Am I listening?

Call on the Angel of Communication when you need to express yourself but you can't seem to find the right words or even imagine being able to say what needs to be said. This angel comes to your aid when you are challenged by the fear of speaking, either in front of large groups or to one specific individual. When working with this angel, use journaling as a tool to sort out what you want to say and to practice different ways to phrase it. Use your imagination to make believe you've already said what needs to be said with ease and grace by using the Angel of Communication as your sounding board. This angel can also help when you feel misunderstood and need to express yourself with more clarity or in a way that will be better received.

Chakras

Heart chakra to communicate with others on a soul-to-soul level. *Solar plexus chakra* to find the courage and confidence to speak your truth. *Third eye chakra* to awaken conscious recognition of and the ability to use telepathy—mind-to-mind and heart-to-heart communication through pictures, feelings, and thoughts. *Throat chakra* to hear, to be heard, and to speak eloquently.

Colors

Dark blue to peacefully express your intuition. *Pastel blue* to hear, know, and see the helpful messages being sent to you. *Purple* to welcome in the vibration of higher consciousness. *Turquoise* to hear and know the music of the celestial realm.

Gemstones

Amazonite to know the truth or when you need to speak the truth. *Amethyst* to employ your intuition when you listen to others speak. *Angelite* to recognize that messages from the other realms come in a variety of ways—for example, as signs in nature, on billboards, or through intuition. *Blue calcite* to help you be more aware of how you say things and what you say so that you can employ "word patrol" when necessary. *Blue lace agate* to listen more closely when others speak and to really hear and understand what they are trying to express. Blue lace agate amplifies the ability to recognize angelic communication. *Lapis lazuli* to maintain a sense of calm and focus during conversations. *Sodalite* to express yourself peacefully. *Turquoise* to listen to the Divine and to allow the Divine to express itself through you.

Essential Oils

Elemi to get in touch with deep feelings and find healthy ways to communicate those feelings. *Eucalyptus* to breathe deeply and relax enough to say what you need to say and listen to what you need to hear. *Geranium* to help you clear out angry thoughts and let go of irritability to establish a good foundation for healthy communication. *Grapefruit* to improve angelic communication. *Hyacinth* to recognize messages from higher realms of consciousness as well as to aid in communication with loved ones on the Other Side. *Ravensara* to open and clear the throat chakra, the gateway to receiving and interpreting communication with the Universe. *Tea tree* to conduct the incoming and outgoing wisdom being communicated through you from higher consciousness and to tap into the vibrations of mind-to-mind communication. *Thyme* to facilitate telepathic communication.

Supportive Archangels

Archangel Gabriel to receive communication from the Divine. *Archangel Haniel* to open your channels of inspiration and awaken your ability to communicate with nature spirits. *Archangel Uriel* to align with ideas, creativity, insights, and universal consciousness.

Suggested Petition

Oh, Angel of Communication! Show me how to take the steps necessary to improve my communication skills. Please help me state my message simply and positively. Help me develop my listening skills and be engaged with the speaker. Allow the tone of my words to be gentle and the manner in which I express myself to be heart centered. As I project my thoughts, let them be well received. Help me be mindful of my body language and expressions while I speak. Please dispel any misinterpretation and increase excellent communication. Thank you!

Affirmations

When I speak, people listen and understand me. I communicate from my heart to the hearts of others. I visualize and send mental pictures as I express my ideas, visions, opinions, and matters of importance. I hear and know what isn't being said through telepathic communication. I am aware of peripheral situations. I pay attention to body language.

ANGEL OF COMPASSION

*D*o I need to be more compassionate and understanding with myself? Am I empathetic when interacting with others? How can I be an instrument of compassion and mercy?

Call on the Angel of Compassion when you observe that you are being less tolerant and more impatient with others. Ask this angel to open your heart and your consciousness so that you can bring comfort and mercy to the people in your life. Call on the Angel of Compassion to help you notice if you need to show yourself more compassion, and set a kindhearted intention to do so. Foster your empathy and mercy by being gentle and warm when you see a fellow human or animal experiencing a hard time. Shine with compassion for anyone who is suffering and help support them on their journey. This angel is the one to turn to when you need to increase and improve how profoundly you care. Let yourself cultivate a willingness to help others with the basics of life by being more thoughtful.

Chakras

Crown chakra to expand your understanding and thereby develop genuine concern for others. *Heart chakra* to feel and know loving kindness. *Root chakra* to take a grounded and realistic approach to helping yourself and others. *Throat chakra* to relieve hostile words and thoughts and shift into kindness.

Colors

Amber yellow to make positive changes from a self-empowered standpoint. *Green* to activate loving kindness and compassion. *Pastel blue* to improve peace and harmony within yourself. *Pink* to feel surrounded by compassion and love.

Gemstones

Chrysoprase to heighten your self-compassion. *Green tourmaline* to activate compassion with Divine love, mercy, and tolerance. *Hiddenite* to improve the balance between your mind and your emotions and to enhance feelings of love for self and others. *Kunzite* to encourage kindness, compassion, and tolerance. *Malachite* to get to the heart of the matter with an open heart and to get an awareness of patterns of interactions and the cycles of life and living. *Morganite* to have the spiritual fortitude to pull yourself or others out of the doldrums and wrap yourself in an energetic blanket of love to work through tough feelings. *Pink calcite* to activate the opening of your heart chakra so that you can release feelings of anger and frustration. *Rhodochrosite* to acquire the qualities of the Divine Feminine. *Rhodonite* to help you connect your mind to your heart. *Rose quartz* to align your consciousness with Divine love, compassion, mercy, tolerance, and kindness. *Sunstone* to shine the light on compassionate action and be an instrument of peace and love to help all humanity.

Essential Oils

Frankincense to align with compassion, inner peace, tolerance, and love. *Jasmine* to be a blessing and spread nurturing vibrations wherever you go. *Lemon* to shine light on the path of the soul's purpose to be compassionate and loving. *Neroli* to reveal the full magnificence of your spirit and exemplify loving kindness. *Sandalwood* to align your body, mind, and spirit with the Divine. *Spikenard* to align with the healing power of inner peace, empathy, and the Divine Feminine.

Supportive Archangels

Archangel Auriel to align with the Divine Mother, who emanates compassion and mercy. *Archangel Chamuel* to guide you through relationship issues that require compassionate action. *Archangel Zadkiel* to develop sympathy and empathy for others' misfortunes.

Suggested Petition

Oh, Angel of Compassion! Come walk by my side so that I can feel, know, and understand the experiences of the human condition. Let me be an instrument to serve humanity through sensitivity and compassion. Help me realign my mind with my heart and let my heart be the center focus of my thought processes. Show me how to be empathetic without enabling dysfunctional behavior or taking on the suffering of others. I want to grow emotionally, mentally, and spiritually mature so that I can be a comfort to others in times of need. Thank you!

Affirmations

I am compassionate and kind. I attract thoughtful, loving people into my life. I focus on empathy and speak with kindness and compassion. Each day, my intention is to live with love and act with compassion and tolerance in every personal encounter. I am aligned with the healing powers of inner peace and kindness. I am able to help others by vibrating love through my presence, words, and actions.

Angel of Creative Intelligence

*I*s there something I've wanted to do that requires me to be creative? Am I inspired to take action to manifest my desires? How can I use my creative intelligence to align with my magnificence?

Call on the Angel of Creative Intelligence when you need to apply your knowledge and your skills to achieve your goals. Let this angel help you tap into your creativity. This angel helps you access your full mental capacity and use your powers of reasoning and ingenuity to produce something unique that originated in your imagination. Whether it is an innovative piece of art, a song, or a meal, this angel helps you access your creativity to cleverly and insightfully bring your ideas into actuality. Ask this angel to increase your self-confidence, especially during times when you aren't feeling very smart or imaginative. Remember, there are always tools to learn new things, so give this angel permission to motivate you to do the research, get training, and develop new skills.

Chakras

Crown chakra to increase intellectual pursuits. *Navel chakra* to take the action required to manifest your inspired thoughts. *Third eye chakra* to amplify intuitive realizations that apply directly to the creative project. *Throat chakra* to be open to receive inspiration from the heavenly realm.

Colors

Light purple to stimulate your imagination and the power of visualization. *Navy blue* to calm mental chatter so that you can hear and know the knowledge available in your consciousness. *Orange* to connect with fresh, creative ideas and actually take action on those ideas. *Pastel green* to be smart enough to realize that you can always discover new information. *Turquoise* to support learning from various cultures and philosophies. *White* to help you clearly translate information as it is downloaded from the Universe into your awareness.

Gemstones

Azurite to help you retrieve information. *Carnelian* to come up with innovative approaches to the task at hand. *Clear quartz* to help you see all situations clearly to enable you to sort through and organize information. *Copper* to serve as a conduit for receiving information. *Fluorite*, the genius stone, to support your brain in thinking through complex problems and situations. *Golden topaz* to surround yourself with people who recognize your intelligence and thoughtfulness. *Herkimer diamond*, the stone of concrete manifestation, to retain information and tap into the pockets of memories and knowledge when needed. *Phantom quartz* to notice the opportunities to learn new things. *Sapphire* to clear away distortions and realize wisdom and truth. *Selenite* to activate your connection with ancient wisdom and knowledge.

Essential Oils

Basil to bring forth creative clarity, untangle chaotic thoughts, and improve memory. *Black pepper* to tap into your source of inspiration and ramp up the physical and energetic endurance to bring your creation forth. *Cinnamon* to unblock energy that seems to be standing in the way of your goals and the completion of creative projects. *Orange* to connect with fresh, creative ideas and to get your creative juices flowing with renewed enthusiasm. *Palmarosa* to expand your mental pathways so that you can more easily generate new ideas. *Petitgrain* to activate creative thought processes and bring forth what you are inspired to create. *Ravensara* to help you access the limitless wellspring of creativity that is available to all.

Supportive Archangels

Archangel Auriel for a healthy mind and an enthusiastic outlook. *Archangel Gabriel* to download the knowledge and wisdom of high-vibration inspiration. *Archangel Metatron*, a heavenly scribe, to activate higher awareness and help you read the Akashic records—the records of all that is, all that was, and all potential future realities. *Archangel Seraphiel* to incorporate your knowledge and information into your daily decisions in a practical manner. *Archangel Uriel* to access creativity, insights, and universal consciousness. *Archangel Zaphkiel* to utilize the power of contemplation to creatively approach situations.

Suggested Petition

Oh, Angel of Creative Intelligence! Please show me how to develop my inner genius. Guide me to educate myself in areas where my knowledge is lacking. Help me tap into the Divine wisdom I need to accomplish whatever I put my mind to. Help me realize that I have much more to learn in this life and that there are many opportunities for growth. Light my path so I can see more clearly and uncover new paths to increase my intelligence and mental capabilities. Thank you!

Affirmations

I am an intelligent being with the ability to focus on complex tasks. I enjoy learning new things. I am smart enough to realize that I can always discover new information. I am organized and create the perfect space in which to learn. I am conscious of my intelligence, and I know how to tap into ancestral knowledge. I complete my tasks and creative projects with ease. I'm self-motivated and productive.

ANGEL OF DETERMINATION

*A*m I determined and focused on achieving the goals I've decided to go after? What makes me feel resolute? Am I unwavering in my purpose?

Call on the Angel of Determination when you've made a decision about some aspect of your life and need extra support to persevere with faith and a strong vision. Throughout life, you will be determined to make something happen with regard to various life situations, but you still need the strength to see it through. This angel can be your ally when you are considering giving up, but know that you must keep going and complete the goal you've set. The Angel of Determination can inspire you to stay focused on your intention by helping you to believe in yourself. Let this angel inspire you to stay determined with single-minded focus so you come out on the other side with good results. When it's time to take action, this angel will help you take the necessary steps to transform your life. You can do anything!

Chakras

Crown chakra to sharpen your clarity of purpose in alignment with your soul's purpose. *Root chakra* to stay grounded but also enthusiastic while pursuing your determined goal. *Third eye chakra* to activate your sixth sense, that which is beyond the physical, to lead you toward completion of your intentions.

Colors

Black for grounding and feelings of safety. *Brown* to root yourself in the work you are doing. *Translucent yellow* for mental clarity and a joyful attitude. *Red* for strength and vitality.

Gemstones

Ametrine to clear your mind, realize your inner power, and maintain focus to stay on course with your decisions. *Bismuth* to maintain focus and a determined effort to succeed. *Blue lace agate* to discover your life's work and fulfill your purpose. *Danburite* to open your heart and empower you to align with the highest and best version of yourself. *Dogtooth calcite* for grounded determination and to gain clarity on what you are doing, where you are going, and how to get there. *Garnet* to align you with your passion for living and your passion for life. *Golden calcite* to improve confidence and clarity regarding your life's passion. *Prasiolite* to strengthen your resolve and your mental fortitude to persevere, and to follow tasks through to completion. *Red calcite* to move forward and take grounded action on your passion and purpose. *Red goldstone* to motivate you to take action with tenacity. *Red tiger's eye* to think outside the box and implement your ideas into action.

Essential Oils

Benzoin for focused thinking and increased action to follow your chosen path. *Bergamot* to increase confidence and mental clarity. *Cinnamon* to venture outside your regular approach to situations and allow for new and different results to manifest. *Thyme* to boost your courage to live in alignment with your soul's contract and agreements.

Supportive Archangels

Archangel Haniel to align with your soul's purpose and the determination to fulfill your purpose. *Archangel Jehudiel* to strengthen your self-control and ability to overcome poor choices. *Archangel Metatron* to activate the connection with higher consciousness and the evolution of your soul. *Archangel Michael* to uncover your inner superpowers to forge forward even if faced with challenging situations. *Archangel Raphael* to strengthen your determination to overcome health challenges. *Archangel Uriel* to fire up and transform inner conflicts, freeing you to take action and move forward.

Suggested Petition

Oh, Angel of Determination! Please help me release impatience, frustration, and disappointment so that I can stay focused on successful outcomes. Offer me strength and help me keep my determination even in the face of setbacks. Provide me with spiritual fortitude, perseverance, and tenaciousness. Help me find the confidence and courage to be self-assured as I eagerly move forward toward my goal. Shine light on my path as I diligently and conscientiously create the reality I know is for the highest good. Thank you!

Affirmations

Power and strength are mine. It is safe for me to be powerful in loving ways. I am determined to achieve my goals and dreams. My clarity and focus are unparalleled, and I have the confidence and courage I need to move forward fearlessly. I've done the work with great skill, and it is time to shine my light and share my gifts with the world.

ANGEL OF DISCERNMENT

*H*ow can I get better at recognizing if someone is being authentic? What might I be missing about a person's character? What do I need to see or realize to fully understand a situation?

Call on the Angel of Discernment when you feel like you need to improve your ability to recognize how people truly are at their core. This angel can be your ally when you feel you can't trust your own judgment when "friending" people or allowing people into your inner circle. The Angel of Discernment can help you realize if someone is a faker or is trying to do something that isn't coming from a place of integrity. Let this angel open your ears to hear and open your eyes to see circumstances and people as they truly are. There are times in life when you are being shown the truth about a person or situation but you are missing it. Use this angel to shine light on what you need to see, hear, or realize in order to discern for yourself who or what you want to align yourself with.

Chakras

Crown chakra to align with Divine light and always be divinely protected. *Navel chakra* to access and trust your gut feelings about situations. *Solar plexus chakra* to have the courage to establish boundaries based on realizations surrounding others' authenticity. *Third eye chakra* to clearly see people for who they truly are and identify any less-than-favorable intentions. *Throat chakra* to speak up for yourself as you realize that you are empowered to take steps to shield yourself from potentially negative situations.

Colors

Purple to quickly transform situations you realize aren't for your highest good. *White* to discern trustworthy people, places, and situations to welcome into your life. *Yellow* to encourage good judgment when interacting with people or considering new opportunities and offers.

Gemstones

Amazonite to discern the truth and set the boundaries with anyone who is not coming from a place of genuineness and integrity. *Amber* to have the courage to set boundaries and make positive changes. *Ametrine* for the courage to set boundaries with others. *Heliodor* to discern the thoughtforms, or the mental energy, circling in your mind that are specifically unhelpful. *Purple-dyed agate* to open your consciousness to unlimited possibilities. *Yellow jasper* to identify what you are feeling and recognize the emotions at play inside you.

Essential Oils

Cardamom to digest life and all that is going on around you, to discern the truth, and to take positive action by using the wisdom of the elders and ancestors. *Lemon* to trust your own inner knowing. *Sandalwood* to acknowledge your intuition and trust your awareness of your own feelings as well as the feelings of others. *Tea tree* to trust your ability to see things and read situations clearly. *Wintergreen* to discern the difference between truth and misperceptions.

Supportive Archangels

Archangel Chamuel to heal from a relationship where a friend or lover was disloyal or hid important information about themselves or their life. *Archangel Gabriel* for a stronger connection to your inner knowing. *Archangel Michael* to protect you from unwanted situations and people who aren't for your highest good. *Archangel Raphael* to heal you in a way that shifts your energy so that you won't attract dishonest people. *Archangel Zadkiel* to have mercy on the people who try to trick or deceive you.

Suggested Petition

Oh, Angel of Discernment! Please help me improve my ability to discern what's best for me. Show me how to be strong and how to align with my highest good in order to avoid what is not good for me. Help me improve my ability to see and know the truth. Help me to know when and how I can keep away unwanted people and situations. Please increase my ability to see through situations earlier in my interactions with others for my highest good. Help me gain clarity in my life. Thank you!

Affirmations

I am very perceptive and discerning in all areas of my life. I see things from varying perspectives. I have good judgment when deciding which people I will allow into my inner circle. I am mindful of being in places that support a loving vibration. I take good care of myself because I know what is good for me.

ANGEL OF DISCIPLINE

*D*o I need more self-control? Am I following the rules and acceptable codes of conduct? Do I practice spiritual discipline on a regular basis?

Call on the Angel of Discipline when you need to improve your ability to follow the reasonable codes of behavior set forth by society. The Angel of Discipline is also the ally to turn to when you want to stay on course with your physical training such as running, biking, strength training, cardio class, Pilates, and similar fitness activities. It's one thing to start a practice, and it is another to have the discipline to continue to practice and improve yourself. This is also the angel to seek assistance from when you want to incorporate consistent spiritual practices into your day. This angel will support you once you've made a clear decision that you want to develop habits that will increase your ability to grow and strengthen your core essence. Enlist the help of the Angel of Discipline when you find yourself in need of more self-control and self-mastery.

Chakras

Crown chakra to know the path of self-mastery and self-awareness. *Root chakra* to stay on task and to be strong and focused. *Solar plexus chakra* to remain aware of your connection to your personal power. *Third eye chakra* to engage your spiritual vision to see yourself carrying out your intentions.

Colors

Red to amplify passion and purpose, thereby helping you to maintain disciplined focus. *Royal blue* to align with integrity, loyalty, and wisdom. *Royal purple* to activate your ability to rise above situations and follow the high road in all circumstances.

Gemstones

Black tourmaline to draw out the negative emotions that cause you to react uncontrollably. *Charoite* to amplify your personal power and sort out chaotic thoughts to make a clear plan and stick to it. *Fluorite* to maintain focus and garner strength and endurance. *Hiddenite* to aid with diplomacy and emotional control in both business and personal pursuits, including weight control. *Red jasper* to remind you to stay focused when you are establishing a new spiritual discipline. *Red tiger's eye* as a grounding force in your spiritual practice to remove the energy of procrastination and add vigor and determination. *Ruby in zoisite* to shift your perceptions to maintain a focus on loving intentions. *Sardonyx*, a stone of great discipline, to ward off distractions to accentuate a stable spiritual practice. *Vanadinite* to help you disintegrate destabilizing emotional states and recompose your thoughts to move forward with discipline.

Essential Oils

Basil to reclaim emotional balance and control. *Geranium* to maintain composure and ownership of your circumstances. *Niaouli* to open your awareness and see your soul's purpose. *Vetiver* to balance your emotions and mindset and to remain focused on your personal goals.

Supportive Archangels

Archangel Ariel for vitality and inspired action. *Archangel Gabriel* for inspired thought and unwavering action. *Archangel Michael* to remove fears and phobias that might distract you from your intentions. *Archangel Sabrael* to ward off distracting, incessant mind chatter. *Archangel Uriel* for wisdom, peace, and higher guidance.

Suggested Petition

Oh, Angel of Discipline! I feel like my life is out of my control. Please help me ward off negative thinking as well as negative people and situations. Enhance my personal power so that I can transform my life and restore mental and emotional balance. I want to let go of chaotic thoughts and confusing situations. Shine light on my thoughts so that I can sort them out and find the path that allows me to stay focused and steadfast while fostering good energy. Show me how to be committed, unwavering, and constant in my efforts and in my life. Thank you!

Affirmations

I understand the factors controlling my life, and I know that I am the one in control. I am disciplined and accountable to myself. I follow through and see my projects to completion. I have willpower and self-control. I am loyal, devoted, dependable, and true.

ANGEL OF DIVINE INTERVENTION

*W*hy do I need help that is beyond ordinary at this time? What miracle would help me? What specific assistance do I need to overcome this current situation?

Call on the Angel of Divine Intervention when a situation looks so dismal that you can't see a way out. This angel can advocate on your behalf to divinely change the likely outcome of a situation. This angel is your messenger when you just don't know what to do, what to say, or how to unravel an old reality and reconstruct a new one. The Angel of Divine Intervention aligns with your consciousness to inspire you with ideas that can show you how to transform a challenging situation into one that is more in alignment with the greatest good for all. Call on this angel for support and then trust in the process and know that heavenly intercession is on your side. Be as specific as possible when requesting Divine intervention, and be sure to give this angel permission to help you in a very specific area of your life.

Chakras

Crown chakra to align with the part of your consciousness where you can tap into miracles. *Heart chakra* to connect with your spiritual essence and create miracles in your life. *Root chakra* to take a grounded approach and cocreate the solutions and actions needed to bring about a desired outcome. *Solar plexus chakra* to remember your magnificence and stand in that power. *Third eye chakra* to use your spiritual powers of visionary realizations to actualize blessings.

Colors

Blue to align with Archangel Michael and his powers of intervention on behalf of the Divine. *Gold* to help connect you with Archangel Uriel to light the way to overcome any challenge. *Iridescent white* to activate your halo at your crown chakra and enhance your connection with the Divine. *Orange* to help you come up with creative solutions to various challenges. *Purple* to transform any issues or challenges through alchemy. *Silver* to know that, in most situations, there is always a positive takeaway.

Gemstones

Amethyst to invite and invoke transformational and miraculous assistance from the highest forces of good. *Copper* to activate a channel or conduit for miracles. *Fire agate* to transform current situations and take an active role in Divine intervention. *Sunstone* to increase light and joy as you improve personal self-confidence. *Pyrite* to ground the experience and be present in the process of the Divine intervening in your life.

Essential Oils

Angelica to attract celestial help when you need someone to intervene on your behalf. *Bergamot* to raise your self-esteem and trust your inner knowing. *Jasmine* to call upon saints and spiritual masters, such as Saint Therese of Lisieux and Mother Mary, to help manifest miracles. *Lavender* to relax in a state of peaceful knowledge that encourages kindness and compassion. *Mandarin* to connect more fully with your Guardian Angel and to remember to ask for specific assistance. *Pink grapefruit* for imaginative clarity to shift your personal vibration into an energy field of pure love. *Rose geranium* to stay focused on your heart and the amazing power of love. *Rosewood* to focus on your good attributes and access the courage to joyfully step forward. *Vetiver* to elicit feelings of safety.

Supportive Archangels

Archangel Gabriel to bring forth miracles through your own inner visions and realizations delivered from the Divine. *Archangel Michael* to provide constant support and protection as your life shifts into a new reality as a result of the Divine intervention. *Archangel Raphael* to provide healing support through the transformation. *Archangel Uriel* to stay on the path of enlightenment and higher wisdom.

Suggested Petition

Oh, Angel of Divine Intervention! I don't know what to do next or how to handle this situation. Please guide the way so that I know the next step to take. Also help me see what I should *not* do with regard to this present situation. Help me find the right words and best course of action. If it is best to do nothing or completely remove myself from the situation, guide me away from the action. Please show me how to proceed by sending symbolic messages and inspiration. Thank you!

Affirmations

I know how to handle any situation that arises. Support from my friends, family, and colleagues guides me when I need the help. Guidance and inspiration from my angels and other spirit guides come to me and I use the messages. Inner realizations are available to me and a normal part of my life. I have the courage to step forward.

ANGEL OF DIVINE REMEMBRANCE

*D*o I remember the Divine on a daily basis? Am I remembered by the Divine? Who do I need to remember in my prayers and what must I remember about myself?

Call on the Angel of Divine Remembrance to remember your Divine spark when you need to place more attention on your spiritual self. Ask this angel to help you tune in not only to the divinity of masters and saints, but your own divinity as well. This angel guides you toward stillness through prayer, contemplation, and meditation. The Divine has not forgotten you, and with a little focus, you haven't forgotten your own connection to the Divine. It is your responsibility to cultivate a relationship with your spiritual nature and remember that you are a spiritual being having a human experience. Review your soul agreements through mindful actions. You have a purpose that you agreed to before your arrival this planet. This angel is your ally when you need to focus your awareness on prayer, inner connection, and purpose. Quiet time away from distractions allows for peaceful remembrance. Know that you are remembered and that others need you to remember them.

Chakras

Crown chakra to enhance your awareness of your spiritual nature. *Heart chakra* to increase heartfelt love and compassion for others during prayer. *Root chakra* to encourage a grounded prayer and meditation experience. *Solar plexus chakra* to have the confidence that you are worthy of fond remembrance by others and the Divine. *Third eye chakra* to have the spiritual clarity to see who needs to be remembered in your prayers.

Colors

Golden yellow to focus on self-realization—the fulfillment of your own potential. *Iridescent white* to achieve a state of self-actualization by cultivating your potentials and living a life of excellence. *Periwinkle blue* to invoke stillness, serenity, and calmness.

Gemstones

Amethyst for calm stability, inner wisdom, and connection with your inner mystic. *Aquamarine* to awaken spiritually and for self-development and inspired thought. *Blue chalcedony* to encourage stillness, inner peace, and goodwill for all. *Celestite* to calm the incessant chatter of the mind and to be open to receiving heavenly communication and guidance. *Clear quartz* to maintain focus and to be a clear channel of love and well-being. *Diamonds* to embrace the strength of character necessary to live to your fullest potential. *Elestial quartz* to invite angelic orchestration to be at play in your life and to remember that you are a conduit of the Divine. *Golden calcite* to access a portal into spiritual truths, realizations, and new perspectives. *Kunzite* to remember your true nature—love.

Essential Oils

Basil for clarity and to encourage a creative approach to self-realization. *Frankincense* for a sense of calm and inner peace and to connect with your inner mystic. *Hyacinth* to open yourself up to the healing energy sent your way through prayer and loving thoughts and to remember to pray for others. *Pink grapefruit* to raise your consciousness to align with a much higher vibration to bring back memories of heaven and lives between lives. *Rose geranium* to nourish your soul and invoke guardians of protection during periods of personal transformation. *Rosemary* for mental and emotional acuity and to be fully present in your daily activities. *Rosewood* to support you in your intention to increase your connection with the Divine.

Supportive Archangels

Archangel Metatron to help you access higher states of consciousness. *Archangel Michael* to encourage you to pray for yourself and for others. *Archangel Zaphkiel* to aid in contemplative thought, mindfulness, and stillness.

Suggested Petition

Oh, Angel of Divine Remembrance! I want to remember my connection with the Divine and all the angels. Please help me remember the spiritual being I am. Help me cultivate my relationship with the Divine through my deeds and actions. Inspire me to pray and to remember others in my prayers. Quiet my mind and inspire me to sit in quiet solitude to deepen my connection with the Divine through contemplation and meditation. Help me to know that I am not forgotten. Thank you!

Affirmations

I notice and use the guidance and inspiration from my angels and spirit guides. I feel the entourage of angels in my life. I know the angels are with me at all times. I am aligned with my true spiritual nature. I take the time to quiet my mind. I enjoy spending time in contemplation, and I remember to pray for myself and others.

ANGEL OF DIVINE TIMING

*D*o I feel like I am missing opportunities? Am I aware of opportunities when they show up? Can I see when messages and guidance are being delivered to me?

Call on the Angel of Divine Timing when you need to improve your ability to recognize a good prospect or a chance to improve your life. This angel is your ally to increase your ability to hear Divine guidance from angels, spirit guides, power animals, fairies, and the Other Side. Divine timing is always available when you exercise your situational awareness and listen more closely when others speak to really hear and understand what they are trying to express. Often the writing is on the wall and guidance is being provided all the time. Pay attention and develop self-trust when reading the cues from the Divine. Allow yourself to recognize this powerful force of timing and Divine orchestration at play and believe that you are always in the right place at the right time with the right people.

Chakras

Crown chakra to align with your connection with the Divine. *Third eye chakra* to listen, see, hear, and know the signs that guide you to be in perfect timing. *Throat chakra* to know exactly when to speak up and when it is best to say nothing.

Colors

Turquoise to activate a balanced throat chakra. *White* to shine light on your path to recognize when it is time to take action.

Gemstones

Amazonite to realize that spiritual help is always available. *Angelite* to imagine that you are in the right place at the right time with the right people. *Blue lace agate* to develop trust of the spiritual realm. *Celestite* to strengthen your connection with the angelic realm and all messengers of the Divine. *Kyanite* to align with higher consciousness and develop higher awareness. *Moonstone* to improve receptivity and intuition. *Selenite* to actively respond to your thoughts, wishes, and dreams according to the Divine plan. *Seraphinite* to facilitate communication with the angelic realm. *Turquoise* to increase reception of the channel of Divine inspiration.

Essential Oils

Allspice to recognize the blessings and network of support that's available to you. *Angelica* to remember and know the existence of the heavenly messengers who assist you in your daily activities. *Frankincense* to open your consciousness to align with your soul's truth. *Grapefruit* to listen to the still, small voice within to find guidance and answers to your self-inquiry questions. *Myrrh* to stabilize your thoughts and focus your attention on the truths that can only be found within. *Thyme* to assist you in aligning with your soul's purpose.

Supportive Archangels

Archangel Haniel for Divine communication, determination, and alignment with your soul's purpose. *Archangel Michael* to attract an entourage of angelic helpers to arrange circumstances for the desired outcome.

Suggested Petition

Oh, Angel of Divine Timing! Please orchestrate my life with me and help me to be mindful of the signs and symbols along my path. Show me the truth. I want to notice when I am at the right place at the right time with the right people. Help me trust my intuition and act upon cues so that I am participating in the Divine orchestration at play in my life. I want to realize my full potential and fulfill my heavenly agreements. Help build my confidence so that I am more open to Divine messages and can see the light illuminating my path. Thank you!

Affirmations

Favorable opportunities present themselves to me in many ways, and I follow through on their promise. I am always in the right place at the right time. I have the blessing of Divine timing, and I am grateful for angelic orchestration at play in my life. Angels provide me with guidance all the time.

ANGEL OF THE DREAMTIME

*W*hat do I want to learn or remember through my dreams? How can I remember, interpret, and understand my dreams? What are my dreams trying to communicate to me?

Call on the Angel of the Dreamtime to be your guide to consciously recall dreams. This angel helps you when you want to remember your dreams that deliver important realizations and information that creates your waking reality. The Angel of the Dreamtime is your guide through the sacred sleep for purposes of regeneration and restoration of your body. Also of great importance is your dreams' ability to help you process life events and work through emotional and mental challenges, thereby allowing for a happier and more balanced life. This angel is extremely important on your spiritual journey and it assists you in your ability to connect with guides and angels as well as ancestors. Ask this angel to help you interpret the meaning of your dreams and apply the information to be inspiration for your waking-life activities. Dreams are important for divination as they provide you with direction to fulfill your life's purpose.

Chakras

Crown chakra to connect with the mystic within you that has access to the records of all that is, all that was, and all potential future realities. *Navel chakra* to have grounded dreams from your center of power. *Third eye chakra* to recall your dreams with clarity. *Throat chakra* to connect with the spiritual realm through various modes of communication.

Colors

Blue for calm energy to invite peace and quiet into your surroundings. *Purple* to reflect on truth through quiet contemplation. *Turquoise* for good communication in all states of awareness. *White* to find peace through inner reflection.

Gemstones

Amazonite to become aware of the truth through the dreamtime. *Amethyst* to keep nightmares at bay and encourage pleasant dreams. *Ammonite* to invite prophetic insight through dreams. *Elestial quartz* to reveal wisdom through an understanding of the mysteries of life. *Herkimer diamond* to open up pockets of memories of dreams to bring them into waking consciousness. *Kambaba jasper* to breathe deeply and feel mellow and at peace. *Lepidolite* to maintain balanced mental and emotional bodies. *Moonstone* to allow for the receptive nature of your consciousness to be revealed. *Orbicular jasper* to spiral into the center of your dreams to know the answers from within. *River rock* to stay centered, grounded, and safe. *Selenite* to reflect on the knowledge and wisdom stored within your bones and muscles and bring them forth through dreams.

Essential Oils

Chamomile to release stress and encourage peaceful sleep. *Lavender* for sound sleep and pleasant dreams. *Mandarin* to strengthen your ability to interpret your dreams. *Melissa* to enter the inner sanctums of intuition, dreaming, and prophecy. *Myrrh* to access prophetic dreams. *Palo santo* for protection during spiritual journeywork to uncover deeper truths. *Ravensara* to step into the mystic within and dream the sacred dream.

Supportive Archangels

Archangel Gabriel to deepen sleep and strengthen dream recall to better interpret dreamtime symbols and messages. *Archangel Metatron* for truth, wisdom, and understanding many-leveled connections. *Archangel Raphael* to invite healing through an understanding of dreams. *Archangel Uriel* to allow for visitations from loved ones on the Other Side during sleep. *Guardian Angel* to watch over you while you sleep.

Suggested Petition

Oh, Angel of the Dreamtime! Please draw me into the center of myself to the place of truth and wisdom. Let me clear my consciousness so that I can receive higher levels of prophetic dreaming and messages from a deeper part of myself. Show me how I can put my awareness on the part of me that is in tune with the mysteries of life. Align me with a strong sense of self and my purpose so that I can actualize my soul's purpose. Thank you!

Affirmations

I embrace my dreams and move actively toward manifesting them. My dreams are filled with ideas and inspiration. I awaken with a clear memory of my dreams and easily interpret them. The insights I receive from dreams bring clarity and understanding to my life. I am grateful for sound sleep and pleasant dreams.

ANGEL OF EMOTIONAL MATURITY

*W*hy do I feel so out of balance emotionally? Am I acting out like a child? What is preventing me from overcoming emotional challenges?

Call on the Angel of Emotional Maturity when you observe yourself acting immature and irrational. This is the angel to ask for help when you realize that you have been treating others disrespectfully because your emotions are out of balance. Ask this angel to be your ally so that you can take a close look at your behaviors and act maturely even when your emotions are running rampant. It is helpful to look at how you have contributed to creating circumstances that have hurt your feelings. Determine if you are experiencing emotional exhaustion due to life changes, a medical condition, overwork, or financial stress. Look at the part you played in the actions of others and their reactions to help you discover how to improve yourself. Take steps to make the shift necessary to be happy. Remember, you create your own reality.

Chakras

Heart chakra to love yourself even when your behaviors are less than appropriate. *Navel chakra* to get to the source of an issue and heal the challenge through inner work. *Root chakra* to be sure your basic needs are met through proper nutrition and hydration.

Colors

Blue to calm down and find inner peace. *Green* to know that you, and everything around you, is love. *Red* to take action to change the situation for the better.

Gemstones

Ametrine to transform uncomfortable emotions and perceptions and strengthen self-confidence. *Ammonite* to spiral into the center of your consciousness to have realizations that will help you move out of your present challenges. *Aquamarine* to identify your feelings and resolve unsettling emotions. *Clear quartz* to gain clarity and understanding. *Elestial quartz* to understand why something is happening and to forge ahead with nonjudgmental clarity. *Howlite* to regain emotional balance by cooling heated emotions and intense pressure during potentially explosive situations. *Kunzite* to amplify loving support from within yourself instead of looking for it from others. *Malachite* to see the truth of the emotional patterns you are creating and to heal them. *Moonstone* to restore emotional balance through self-observation and self-reflection. *Pink calcite* to help you find ways to nurture yourself and feel better about life. *Smoky quartz* to eliminate doubt and worry when you are faced with chaos and/or confusion. *Unakite* to find emotional balance by ridding yourself of repetitive negative thought patterns.

Essential Oils

Black pepper to improve your self-worth and self-esteem by burning away negative emotions. *Myrrh* to heal, stabilize, and sedate rampant emotions and cauterize energetic wounds from trauma. *Neroli* to elicit courage and mental strength during challenging times and to bring about inner peace and calm for a quiet mind. *Palo santo* to draw out dark, negative emotions so that they can be released. *Pine* to help protect you from absorbing other people's emotions. *Ravensara* to scramble and release your unconscious broadcast of negative programs. *Rosemary* to clear out negative emotions and paranoia. *Spikenard* to calm and balance your emotions, thereby increasing your emotional maturity. *Sweet marjoram* to calm hysteria and release paranoia and fears, both conscious and subconscious.

Supportive Archangels

Archangel Auriel to assist in the connection with the Divine Feminine to release conscious and subconscious fears. *Archangel Raphael* to help you understand how you created your present situation as well as how to heal it. *Archangel Michael* to protect you from your own chaotic emotions and your potential to permanently damage relationships. *Archangel Muriel* to rebalance your emotions.

Suggested Petition

Oh, Angel of Emotional Maturity! I am having a hard time getting out of my own way with the emotions I am feeling. Please prevent me from lashing out at the people who care for me. Show me how to be mindful so I don't hurt others with my emotional hysteria. Keep me from being emotionally immature and help me shift my perspectives so that I can heal this emotional issue once and for all. Show me what I can do to help myself live a life free from emotional baggage. Give me the clarity I need so that I no longer blame others for problems in my life. Help me take responsibility for my actions as well as my lack of action. Thank you!

Affirmations

My emotions are balanced. Events from my past positively affect my present and future because I have released any negative emotional charge and see only the lessons learned. I am able to identify my feelings and resolve unsettling emotions. Negativity flows away effortlessly and lovingly. I am free of emotional baggage. I fully appreciate this transformation and enjoy emotional maturity.

ANGEL OF ENVY AND JEALOUSY

*A*re people jealous of your success or happiness? Are you being bullied in person or on social media because others feel lack when they see your accomplishments? Are you experiencing the negative effects of jealous behavior? Or are you jealous of someone else?

Call on the Angel of Envy and Jealousy to support you when jealous behavior shows up in your life. This angel can help release resentful behavior when someone takes action to hurt your reputation or business. The Angel of Envy and Jealousy can help you handle either your own envious feelings or when others reveal hateful behavior. When this happens, focus within and pray. Pray that you will be divinely protected and pray, too, for the person who is envious of you. Often, reactions such as envy and jealousy arise from low self-esteem and lack of self-love. This angel reminds you to send blessings to those who have jealousy issues and to wish them well energetically. This angel also helps you avoid mistakenly or consciously sending hurtful vibes back to them. Call on the wisdom within you to recognize that they will face the karmic repercussions and send good vibes their way to help them gain perspective on their inappropriate behaviors.

Chakras

Heart chakra to cultivate love even in situations where others' behavior is hurtful. *Third eye chakra* to gain clarity on how you can improve the manner in which you present yourself to lessen feelings of jealousy. *Throat chakra* to tap into wisdom and grace to manage your responses to challenges.

Colors

Chartreuse green or *olive* to counterbalance envious behavior in yourself or others. *Pink* to encourage feelings of love and compassion for yourself and others. *Yellow* to amplify self-esteem and confidence to overcome the energy of the hater.

Gemstones

Black tourmaline to shield you from the effects of jealousy, yours and others. *Epidote* to dissolve envy—yours of others' blessings or theirs of your good fortune and hard work. *Golden calcite* to maintain focus, clarity, and high self-esteem even when others try to distract you with resentful or troublesome behavior. *Green tourmaline*, also known as *verdelite*, to keep your focus on your goals and your life's work without distraction from haters or envious people. *Heliodor* to become consciously aware of your thoughts, discard the outdated thoughts, and replace them with thoughts that focus on the life you want to live. *Jade* to focus on the blessings in your life. *Kunzite* to help you overcome the negative effects of bullying and hateful behavior. *Peridot* to transform negative emotions like self-sabotage, jealousy, agitation, and impatience into lighter emotions such as love, compassion, acceptance, and gratitude. *Prasiolite* to integrate and process situations so you can rise above others' challenging behaviors. *Rose quartz* to maintain a focus on blessings, love, tolerance, kindness, and compassion. *Selenite* to help dissipate feelings of inadequacy, jealousy, doubt, fear, and other types of negativity. *Tiger's eye*, historically associated with keeping away the evil eye, to repel jealousy and the bad intentions of others. *Tourmalinated quartz* to clear negative mental energy associated with jealousy, negative self-talk, confusing mental chatter, and general chaos. *Yellow jasper* to increase courage to step away from people who are resentful of your good fortune and your destiny.

Essential Oils

Basil to ward off jealousy, set boundaries, and amplify your personal power. *Celery seed* for overcoming your insecurities and the jealousy of others or when you need to have the courage to set boundaries with others. *Clove* to deflect jealousy and for protection against ill wishes and negative energy from others as well as from yourself. *Geranium* for protection and deflection from negative thoughts and beliefs. *Lavender* to deter other people's jealousy and negative energies. *Palo santo* to draw out negative emotions, heal emotional problems, and reduce anxiety. *Rosemary* for deflecting negativity and jealousy and calming paranoid thoughts.

Supportive Archangels

Archangel Michael to inspire others to come to your defense and counteract negative comments and falsehoods. *Archangel Raphael* to heal your emotions and your feelings during and after bullying-type experiences. *Archangel Sabrael* to deter jealousy and negative forces. *Archangel Zadkiel* to help you feel compassion, forgiveness, and mercy for those who have been unkind to you.

Suggested Petition

Oh, Angel of Envy and Jealousy! Please help me relieve hurt feelings when others have treated me unkindly due to their jealousy. Release their envy of my good fortune and help them realize that it takes passionate dedication over the years to become successful. Inspire me to improve the manner in which I interact with others and open my heart to send loving kindness toward those who feel insecure or lacking. Help them get the attention they need in a positive way so that they don't resort to hurting others for attention. Help me know and remember that good fortune and blessings are often the result of years of good thoughts, conscious deeds, and hard work. Open my heart to develop my capacity to love and admire others' success. Thank you!

Affirmations

I attract secure people. My thoughts and actions create beneficial results. My friends, family, and colleagues are happy for my good fortune, and I am happy for theirs. I know that good fortune is the result of positive thoughts and energy. I have an open heart and send out warm vibes for others' well-being and success. I am grateful for all the blessings I have as well as for those still yet to come.

ANGEL OF FERTILITY

*A*m I ready and willing to be a parent? Is there an idea that I want to give birth to? Do I bring life to my visions and ideas?

Call on the Angel of Fertility to support you when you want to have a child or when you want to cultivate a fertile mind to conceive a good idea. Being fertile for reproduction is only one aspect of fertility. The other is to have a fertile mind capable of developing great ideas and birthing them into reality. This angel assists you through the process of producing offspring by first helping you recognize that birthing a child and becoming a parent begins even before conception. Preparing to bring a child into the world is a sacred act, and this angel can aid in conscious conception on all levels, including preparing yourself mentally, emotionally, physically, and spiritually. You can also turn to this angel when you are ready to give birth to your creative ideas. Manifesting what you create in your imagination takes great courage and long-term dedication. Whether you want to be fertile to carry life or an idea, this angel is your ally.

Chakras

Crown chakra to connect with the spirit of your future child or to birth great ideas with your imagination. *Heart chakra* for heart-centered consciousness in all that you produce. *Navel chakra* to have the courage and emotional balance to create your reality. *Root chakra* for a fertile body and to maintain a grounded approach to your creations.

Colors

Blue to maintain a sense of peace and calm and improve communication with your future child or creative project. *Orange* to initiate creative action. *Yellow* for clarity to hold the vision and bring it into reality.

Gemstones

Botswana agate to cultivate abstract thinking and creative thoughts and to bring your intentions to fruition. *Carnelian* to aid in taking the necessary actions to bring forth your creations through self-motivation. *Clear quartz* to maintain a clear vision for fertility, creativity, family blessings, a happy home, and a healthy body. *Fire agate* to boost creativity, sexuality, and the ability to take action required to manifest your desires. *Orange agate* for grounded determination to actualize your intentions. *Orange calcite* to foster a fertile life. *Ruby* to increase passion, vitality, and sexuality. *Ruby in zoisite* to move the mind into action, to create a passion for life, and to maintain a healthy state through your physical body.

Essential Oils

Anise seed for setting an intention to be fertile and making a step toward conscious parenting before conception. *Clary sage* to release stress and bring about a sense of serenity. *Geranium* to renew health and strength. *Lavender* to calmly focus on your intentions. *Neroli* to release subconscious fears, to elicit courage and mental strength, and to enhance sexual response. *Pine* to improve fertility. *Sage* to balance female reproductive hormones and to ease the challenges of infertility. *Spikenard* to activate the vibration of the Divine Mother for support in overcoming birthing difficulties. *Ylang-ylang* for stress reduction and to stimulate sexual desire.

Supportive Archangels

Archangel Ariel for general health and vitality. *Archangel Gabriel* to guide the unborn child or for the birth of creative inspiration as manifest reality. *Archangel Haniel* to open channels to Divine communication and to align with your soul's purpose. *Archangel Melchizedek* to shine light on your path for your journey here on Earth. *Archangel Muriel* for balanced emotions.

Suggested Petition

Oh, Angel of Fertility! Please help me do the right things to have a fertile body, mind, and spirit. Show me what to do to maintain balanced emotions, improve my creative spirit, and awaken the life force within me. I request that my hormones become rebalanced and that my mental and emotional states are healthy and aligned with the greatest good. Align me with my unborn child or for the conception of the creative inspiration as my imagination becomes manifest reality. Help me to embrace my imagination and be self-motivated and productive. Thank you!

Affirmations

I am fertile in body, mind, and soul. My body is ripe to give birth, figuratively or literally. Vital life force flows vibrantly through me. I am strong and healthy. I am extremely creative and imaginative and able to think abstractly. I am enthusiastic and confident. Creative thoughts are constantly coming to me. I'm self-motivated and productive, so my creative endeavors always come to fruition when I choose to give birth to them.

ANGEL OF FLEXIBILITY

*A*m I being too rigid in my behavior? How can I be more flexible and just go with the flow? What is preventing me from relaxing into this situation?

Call on the Angel of Flexibility when you need to compromise in order to grow with the circumstances that are occurring around you. This angel will help you shift your outlook so that you are more willing to work with the situation and bend in ways you mistakenly thought would break you. The Angel of Flexibility is a good ally when you are having a hard time coping with the situation and feel set in your ways. Be open to receiving inspiration on creative ways to shift your consciousness to be more spacious and accepting of change. With this angel supporting you, practice physical flexibility exercises like stretching, yoga, tai chi, or Pilates with the intention that these practices will give you more flexibility mentally, emotionally, and physically. The Angel of Flexibility and the Angel of Change work well together, so ask them to team up for your greatest good.

Chakras

Navel chakra to activate your willingness to take action to make necessary changes with a relaxed attitude. *Solar plexus chakra* for the confidence and courage to accept the unknown and go with the flow.

Colors

Orange to embrace the present moment and to use changes to spark a new outlook. *Yellow* to be optimistic on an emotional and mental level.

Gemstones

Azurite-malachite to release ego and arrogance. *Blue calcite* to maintain a sense of calm when you communicate with others during times of change. *Leopardskin jasper* for the ability to shift into new patterns and seize opportunities in a changing landscape. *Orange calcite* to embrace taking action in a different way than you usually would.

Essential Oils

Allspice to relax your mind enough to consider ideas for change. *Bergamot* to create new pathways in your mind and brain for more flexibility. *Chamomile* to relieve stress, calm frayed nerves, and generate spiritual connection in the face of changing circumstances. *Clary sage* to remain calm and to encourage a sense of well-being. *Vetiver* to feel grounded and balanced.

Supportive Archangels

Archangel Auriel to release subconscious fears of change. *Archangel Chamuel* for the ability to easily and eagerly compromise in relationships. *Archangel Thuriel* to encourage spending time in nature to relax and be more flexible.

Suggested Petition

Oh, Angel of Flexibility! Please come here now and help me release rigidity around the current situation so that I can relax and accept the present. Show me how to maintain balance as I stretch my range of acceptance of the ever-changing realities of life. Help me be flexible enough to see different ways of handling the relationships in my life so that we are all happy with each other. Help me see that there is more than one way to do something. Thank you!

Affirmations

I am flexible and adaptable. I objectively observe circumstances and seize new opportunities as situations naturally shift and change in my life. I bend and flex with the flow of life around me. There is no resistance, only willingness to go with the flow. I recognize that change always brings about better life situations.

ANGEL OF FORGIVENESS

*W*ho do I want to forgive? Do I need to forgive myself for things I've done to myself or to others? Where is my compassion and mercy?

Call on the Angel of Forgiveness when you are working on showing compassion or mercy toward someone, including yourself. This angel helps you to understand the power of forgiveness and the healing potential of repentance, gratitude, and acceptance. Look to this angel to guide you toward sincere apology for your wrongdoings and to shine light on how you may have contributed to another's unjust actions toward you. Find the way to express gratitude for those experiences, as they have given you an opportunity to grow. Repentance is powerful, and so is gratitude and love. Use gratitude and love to help you embrace your ability to forgive yourself and others. There is always a silver lining within any challenge. Let this angel shine light on the good that is always found within, even if the act of repentance and forgiveness initially feels negative and hard to overcome.

Chakras

Heart chakra for compassion, love, and gratitude for all of life's experiences. *Navel chakra* to process and deal with the emotions underlying the need for forgiveness. *Solar plexus chakra* to heal the bruise to your ego and self-esteem and to release deeper hurt.

Colors

Pastel blue to encourage calm verbal interactions and good communication. *Pink* for self-care, self-love, and the ability to open your heart to allow healing to take place. *Purple* to transform negative situations and to align with compassion and understanding. *Seafoam green* to bring peace, calm, and tranquility to the situation.

Gemstones

Amethyst to release anger and resentment toward someone or yourself for offensive words, actions, or mistakes. *Chrysoprase* to elicit feelings of compassion. *Hiddenite* to foster mental peace and serenity so that you can focus on what is truly important. *Kunzite* to encourage kindness, compassion, and tolerance. *Malachite* to choose and attract patterns of love, compassion, and kindness. *Peridot* to transform hurt feelings and to rise into lighter emotions such as love, compassion, acceptance, and gratitude. *Rhodochrosite* to see the silver lining in any situation and to find the positive that comes out of even negative situations. *Rose quartz* to neutralize negative or resentful feelings toward yourself and others. *Selenite* to detach from drama and gain a greater understanding of people and situations in order to experience more compassion, mercy, and forgiveness. *Sugilite* to see the bigger picture and to deflect negative thoughts from others and from yourself.

Essential Oils

Cedarwood to inspire you to be reflective and prayerful to gain a higher perspective and a deeper understanding of the truth. *Elemi* to help you detach from that which is no longer for your highest good while maintaining a sense of calm and surrender during vulnerable times. *Hyacinth* to help relieve raw feelings of heartache, to release resentment, and to allow for forgiveness. *Palo santo* to transform situations in a shamanic manner and to invoke your ancestors to join forces with you to help you through this period of time. *Pine* to heal, nurture, restore, and forgive and forget the past. *Sage* to clear away residual resentment that could be buried deep within your consciousness. *Sweet marjoram* to calm out-of-balance emotions due to feeling that someone has done something to hurt you on any level—mentally, emotionally, physically, or spiritually.

Supportive Archangels

Archangel Sabrael to release jealousy and negative forces such as retribution. *Archangel Zadkiel* to invoke compassion, mercy, and forgiveness and to have the ability to align with gratitude for having had the experience.

Suggested Petition

Oh, Angel of Forgiveness! Help me open my heart to find a way to release hurt feelings over past challenges, hurtful actions, and conflicts. Let the emotional release rid me of potentially poisonous feelings such as resentment, anger, grief, and deep sadness. Help me to have compassion for others so I can forgive and let go of the past. Guide me to feel gratitude for having had the experience so I can embrace lessons learned. Thank you!

Affirmations

I forgive and forget past injustices. I know that intense feelings of anger, sorrow, and grief will pass when I no longer hold on to them. I release resentment and rage from my body, mind, and spirit. I open myself up to the healing energy of love.

ANGEL OF FUN AND PLAY

*W*hat would make me happy today? What activity makes me feel like I'm having fun? When was the last time I felt playful?

Call on the Angel of Fun and Play when you realize that you've been too serious and you might be working too hard. This angel encourages you to pause to enjoy life more fully and to remember how to have fun. When you were a child, playing was an important part of the development of your brain, body, and social skills. As an adult, play is a key part of maintaining a healthy body, mind, and spirit. Having fun is the perfect tool to relieve toxic stress and support your emotional resilience. A little bit of make-believe and pretend play stimulates your creativity and your imagination, which ultimately fuels great ideas and the ability to see different perspectives in life. It also improves your adaptability and problem-solving skills. Ask the Angel of Fun and Play to help you find more joyful ways to cope with the issues of daily life.

Chakras

Heart chakra to be joyful. *Navel chakra* to enhance creative, joyful expression. *Solar plexus chakra* to activate your core of happiness and playfulness.

Colors

Orange to playfully express yourself through creative action. *Pink* to feel joy and love. *Yellow* for a positive outlook and enthusiasm.

Gemstones

Bloodstone to creatively and playfully pursue your true passion. *Brown agate* to gently keep you on task while still allowing the energy of fun, play, and creativity to surround you. *Citrine* to amplify happiness, joy, and a positive outlook on life. *Cobra jasper* to encourage a reconnection with nature and taking the time to play with animals. *Elestial quartz* to invite angels into your playtime and encourage cosmic coincidence. *Honey calcite* to take the time to enjoy the sweetness of life. *Orange calcite* to encourage action and play. *Rhodonite* to find balance through play, exercise, and laughter.

Essential Oils

Bergamot to generate feelings of joy and happiness. *Geranium* to enjoy the blessing of playful friendships. *Ginger* to relieve apathy and increase passionate action. *Lemon* to think positively and restore vitality. *Lime* for clarity and to experience delight. *Mandarin* to make joyfulness a normal part of your life. *Petitgrain* for confidence and action. *Sage* for feelings of euphoria.

Supportive Archangels

Archangel Ariel to imbue you with the vim and vigor needed to enjoy playing. *Archangel Jophiel* to help you relax and see the beauty in life. *Archangel Thuriel* to inspire outdoor playtime in nature and with animals.

Suggested Petition

Oh, Angel of Fun and Play! I want to take the much-needed time to relax and play. Please inspire me to find creative ways to relax and use my imagination. Stimulate my mind to carve out leisure time and activate my body to engage in fun, rejuvenating play the way I did as a child. Fuel my imagination to create situations that help me forget about work and commitments for a while. Let me feel good about goofing off, sharing jokes, and experiencing a day of fun with no specific goal or destination. Help me give myself permission to play joyfully. Thank you!

Affirmations

I find balance in my life through play, work, rest, exercise, and laughter. I am filled with lightness and joy. I am happy, whole, and complete. I find pleasure and delight in even the small blessings in my life. I love to smile and laugh! I enjoy playing outdoors and spending time in nature. I take in the sweetness of life.

ANGEL OF GOOD FORTUNE

*I*n what ways am I lucky? Where in my life do I feel unlucky? What is the source of all the happiness, luck, and favorable outcomes I've experienced?

Call on the Angel of Good Fortune when you feel like unlucky, like nothing is going your way. This angel can help you change your mind so you can change your luck. After all, you create your reality with your thoughts and beliefs. Ask the Angel of Good Fortune to help you shift your mindset so you can believe that you are always blessed with favorable outcomes and that you can always have great luck! Luck appears to come by chance, but in truth, it is a state of mind. When you believe you can have success, prosperity, and good health along with a wonderful family and good friends—things that make you feel lucky—you invite these things to manifest in your life. Having good fortune is your decision, and the Angel of Good Fortune can help you stay mindful of how lucky you really are.

Chakras

Navel chakra to realize and actualize creative ideas. *Root chakra* to align with a strong, healthy foundation on which you allow blessings to unfold. *Third eye chakra* to see life from a greater perspective with the ability to visualize and imagine various potential realities.

Colors

Gold to illuminate the success, prosperity, and good health you already enjoy. *Green* to attract and maintain favorable situations wherever you may be. *Orange* to creatively imagine how you can attract beneficial, advantageous opportunities and shift or change to achieve desired outcomes. *Purple* to realize that you always have the ability to transform any situation and alchemize it into something that benefits everyone involved.

Gemstones

Amethyst to attract good thoughts, pleasant dreams, and transformational experiences that lead you to blessings and good fortune. *Carnelian* to take the action required to manifest a life filled with all that is good. *Citrine* to look at life optimistically as you consciously create your reality filled with blessings. *Clear quartz* for mental clarity and a balanced attitude to create a life of good fortune and opportunity. *Copper* to be a conduit of good luck for those around you. *Emerald* to maintain solid, financially secure savings. *Golden calcite* to clearly see the path of joy and happiness. *Goldstone* in blue, green, or red to activate the sparkling vibrations of blessings in your life. *Green aventurine*, the shamrock of the gemstone kingdom, to increase the vibration of good luck. *Green tourmaline* for wealth and financial intelligence to manage your prosperity. *Jade* for blessings, good health, great wealth, and happiness. *Orange calcite* to help you with creative visualization skills. *Pyrite* to attract golden rays of blessings and well-being to light your path.

Essential Oils

Bergamot to amplify self-confidence and raise self-esteem to attract beneficial situations. *Cinnamon* to take confident action to attract prosperity and abundance. *Orange* to call in the energy of vitality, freshness, creativity, and joy. *Patchouli* to attract both love and money. *Pine* to protect you from others' negative energy and to keep your mind and space clear and clean. *Rosemary* to be fully present in your daily activities with mindful awareness of opportunities. *Sage* to keep you safe and out of harm's way and to help you transform the mental composition of your thoughts.

Supportive Archangels

Archangel Gabriel to inspire and guide you through symbols and dreams. *Archangel Jophiel* to align you with the wisdom stored within you. *Archangel Michael* to oversee fairness in all situations. *Archangel Sachiel* for good fortune and beneficial outcomes in legal matters. *Archangel Uriel* to increase the light within and around you, thereby attracting golden blessings sparkling down around you.

Suggested Petition

Oh, Angel of Good Fortune! Please help me attract blessings, abundance, prosperity, great health, and happiness into my life. Inspire me to be fortunate enough to know how to create my own luck. In addition to random chance, show me ways to take action to create favorable outcomes and good fortune. Let me manifest my dreams to bring blessings into my own life and into the lives of others. Help me to have plenty of all that is good so that I can share that good fortune with my friends, family, and the community. Thank you!

Affirmations

I am so incredibly lucky! My life is replete with blessings. The energies of abundance and prosperity flow continuously in my life. I am grateful for all that I have. I am safe and secure because luck is on my side. I am blessed with good luck while traveling. My heart is open and I have good fortune when it comes to loving relationships. My creative mind finds ways to generate my own good luck.

ANGEL OF GRATITUDE

*W*hat am I feeling grateful for in my life, past and present? Do I feel as if I am blessed? What are the blessings I am thankful for?

Call on the Angel of Gratitude when you need a little help realizing all the blessings in your life. Ask this angel to help you maintain a focus on all the things you feel grateful for, rather than on the areas you feel are lacking. To establish a gratitude practice, start by writing a list of the people, places, and things that make you feel grateful. Visualize them and send feelings of gratitude and good vibes their way. Take the opportunity to replace thoughts of worry, fear, and anger with thoughts of blessings and appreciation. Use your commute time to count your blessings—just make sure to stay present as you drive, for safety. You can start by having gratitude for your transportation and the financial ability to access it. Then continue to align your awareness with thankfulness and appreciation for all things, both big and small.

Chakras

Crown chakra to align your consciousness with higher awareness. *Heart chakra* for focus on love and blessings.

Colors

Green to maintain an awareness of how lucky you are. *Purple* to transform any challenging thoughts and feelings while focusing on gratitude. *White* for clarity, pure thoughts, and connection with higher consciousness.

Gemstones

Apophyllite for a clear mind and the ability to stay focused on all that is good. *Clear quartz* for mental clarity and self-acceptance so you can be grateful for who you are and what you do. *Green aventurine* to recognize the many blessings in your life and acknowledge your incredibly good fortune. *Herkimer diamond* for a clear understanding of what makes you feel thankful. *Kunzite* to be aware of all the love that surrounds you and how you can radiate love. *Morganite* to be aware of your comforts, abundant wealth, and limitless love. *Rose quartz* to remember to feel grateful for all that you experience.

Essential Oils

Benzoin for focus, clarity, inner peace, and a grateful attitude. *Cedarwood* for a grounded, heartfelt spiritual approach focused on gratitude. *Frankincense* to align with, and feel grateful for, your spiritual nature. *Grapefruit* to sharpen your memory of all the good you've already been blessed with. *Lavender* to relax into the feeling of being blessed with the good things in life. *Ylang-ylang* to maintain a constant feeling of gratitude.

Supportive Archangels

Archangel Michael to have the support you need to stay focused on pleasant memories and everyday blessings, as well as extraordinary reasons to feel gratitude. *Archangel Thuriel* to invite the realization of how interconnected all life is and how nature, plants, and animals are a major reason to be grateful.

Suggested Petition

Oh, Angel of Gratitude! Please help me recognize all the good things in my life so that I can freely express my heartfelt gratitude. Help me to maintain a constant focus of being grateful during my daily activities. Raise my awareness to enable me to see how blessed I am in both big and small ways. Give me the strength to maintain my attention on all that is good and deflect my awareness away from anything that is not. Thank you!

Affirmations

I am so grateful for everything that life has provided for me and for my loved ones. I am thankful for the myriad blessings in my life but especially for my loving friends and family. I have gratitude that all my basic needs are met and are in abundant supply. I can easily identify all that I have to be grateful for, including the things I sometimes take for granted like food, water, and shelter.

ANGEL OF GRIEF

*W*ho or what am I grieving? Am I allowing myself to fully feel my feelings? Why do I feel unable to cry or to stop crying?

Call on the Angel of Grief when you are in the depths of sorrow. While it is natural to dive deep into sadness after the passing of a loved one (including furry and feathered friends), at the end of a relationship, or during a career transition, it is also essential to seek solace and comfort to help you through it. The Angel of Grief is the perfect companion to take with you as you navigate the grieving process and find yourself in its various stages, including shock, denial, pain, anger, depression, loneliness, and acceptance. When you've lost someone, the "year of firsts" is a time when your Angel of Grief can spiritually hold your hand and be at your side as you face your first year of holidays, celebrations, and events without your loved one. Allow this angel to guide your path through the grieving process toward hope and renewal.

Chakras

Crown chakra to find a way to make the experience of grief a truly spiritual experience. *Heart chakra* to fully experience the depth of love for the person, animal, or thing that is being grieved. *Throat chakra* to find a way to express grief and feel support from celestial beings during the grieving process.

Colors

Black to mourn the loss of someone or something that has moved on to the next level of existence. *Purple* for support and healing when one is transitioning from one state of being to another. *White* to symbolize purity and rebirth.

Gemstones

Amethyst to transform and transmute challenging feelings and situations. *Apache tears* to give yourself permission to cry and feel the depth of your feelings. *Apophyllite* for spiritual connection through your mind and heart. *Brucite* to allow the tears to flow when emotions arise. *Celestite* to connect with angels for comfort and to receive communication from the Other Side. *Indigo gabbro*, also known as *merlinite*, to help manage and sort through the mishmash of feelings. *Rhodonite* to let your heart feel sad and still feel love at the same time. *Selenite* for clarity of truth and a deeper understanding of the impermanence of all life.

Essential Oils

Benzoin to reduce or prevent situational depression and stimulate comfort and joy. *Hyacinth* to heal from deep grief associated with losing a loved one. *Lime* to see grief as a pathway to a new chapter that's ready to unfold. *Mandarin* to transform your reality into one of joy and happiness. *Neroli* to clear out toxic thoughts and painful emotions. *Orange* to bring joy and feelings of comfort to children and adults alike. *Vanilla* to flood your consciousness with comforting waves of warm memories.

Supportive Archangels

Archangel Chamuel for relationship healing and to encourage happiness and harmony. *Archangel Melchizedek* to help correct unpleasant endings and to provide insights and esoteric understanding. *Archangel Raphael* to assist you in the healing process of grief. *Archangel Zadkiel* to allow forgiveness and repentance when the situation calls for it and for comfort, mercy, and well-being.

Suggested Petition

Oh, Angel of Grief! Please be at my side to support me during my period of bereavement. Help me feel the sadness and adjust to this different way of life. Help me sort through my various emotions as I experience them. See me through the normal fluctuating states of confusion, denial, relief, abandonment, betrayal, acceptance, and hope. Help the stress of sorrow flow out of my body through my tears so that I can release what has been lost to me on an emotional and physiological level. Thank you!

Affirmations

I completely embrace all of my feelings and bring them to the surface so that I can experience them for what they are and allow them to move on. Feelings of anger, sorrow, and grief will pass as I release them from my body. I open myself up to the healing energy of the love and prayers that others send to me during my grieving period. I have hope.

ANGEL OF A HAPPY HOME

*W*hat makes my home a happy home? What is important to bring me happiness? Is there anything, physical or otherwise, in my home that is preventing it from being a happy one?

Get clear on what makes you feel happy in your home. Make a list of exactly what that happy home will look like and feel like, then ask the Angel of a Happy Home to help you make that vision a reality. Consider if that home will include space for animal companions, how you define your style of furniture and decor, and how you want your yard and garden to appear. Happiness is a choice, and it starts within your own consciousness. Companionship and interactions with others are integral to a positive experience in life, so envision a space that will promote positive life circumstances. Some elements of happiness you may want to bring into your home are a sense of harmony, good communication, and loving kindness between all who enter that space. An abundance of food, money, blessings, good health, feelings of safety, and love are vital components. This angel wants all of this for you.

Chakras

Heart chakra for love as the center for your household. *Navel chakra* for the energy of the womb, hearth, and home. *Root chakra* to restore a strong foundation. *Solar plexus chakra* for the experience of integrating feelings of joy, pleasure, and positivity.

Colors

Blue for inner peace. *Brown* for grounded awareness and feelings of contentment. *Green* to appreciate the pleasures of life and allow for feelings of gratitude and good luck. *Orange* to amplify feelings of contentment and joy. *Pink* to feel comfort and pleasure. *Yellow* for joy and clarity.

Gemstones

Blue lace agate to freely express yourself in your own sacred space and to really hear and understand what others are trying to express. *Black tourmaline* to increase feelings of safety, security, and love. *Clear quartz* to support your overall well-being and to increase your ability to be successful in all endeavors. *Dalmatian jasper* to increase comfort and happiness for animal companions in and around your home. *Green aventurine* for an abundance of food, money, and blessings. *Green moss agate* to enjoy the healing and nurturing power of nature in your own backyard. *Jade* for good health, good luck, great wealth, abundance in all areas of life, and joy. *Kunzite* to emanate love and well-being in a wide circumference around you and your home. *Lapis lazuli* for harmony, protection, and peace. *Petrified wood* to assist in the process of clearing out clutter. *Rose quartz* for loving kindness and to make your space a nurturing environment. *Selenite* to align you with the highest good for all concerned. *Tree agate* for a connection with nature, your yard, and your garden.

Essential Oils

Amber to connect with positive changes and to bring comfort into the household. *Cardamom* to protect the boundaries of your sacred space and to keep unwelcome energies from interfering. *Cinnamon* to encourage a steady flow of strength, warmth, prosperity, and abundance into your home. *Coriander* to invite blessings and extraordinary good health to all who live under your roof. *Lemon* to encourage clean and bright spaces throughout the home and to increase feelings of confidence, mental clarity, and safety. *Pine* to encourage keeping a clean home. *Vanilla* to instill a sense of calm and to invoke feelings of safety and peace in your home.

Supportive Archangels

Archangel Chamuel for healthy and happy relationships in your home environment. *Archangel Jophiel* to help you create a beautiful space for yourself. *Archangel Michael* for constant protection and fairness. *Archangel Raphael* for good health for all who live in your home and all who enter it.

Suggested Petition

Oh, Angel of a Happy Home! I am calling on you to help me create the sacred space in my house or apartment to make it a happy home. Keep everyone in my home healthy and safe. Please show me how to realign my mental and emotional states to gain clarity and focus on what I need to do to create a loving space and environment for myself and those who live with me. Please bestow my home with blessings of happiness, abundance, and harmony. Thank you!

Affirmations

I am grateful for a safe and comfortable place to call home. Only kind and loving people enter my space. It's so nice to have a home filled with love, joy, and happiness. I enjoy my outside space, whether it is as large as a yard with a garden or as small as a windowsill. Feelings of well-being and loving kindness permeate my wonderful home on a daily basis.

ANGEL OF HEALTH

$\mathcal{A}$m I healthy in body, mind, and spirit? Do I need to improve my physical condition? How can I welcome better health into all areas of my life?

Call on the Angel of Health to light the way to a balanced emotional state and a peaceful mind as well as better physical health. Well-being is your natural state. Living a healthy life includes social well-being as well as physical, emotional, and mental balance. Spiritual fulfillment also contributes to good health. Imagine yourself full of health and vitality. Visualize yourself feeling and looking physically fit with plenty of energy—enough energy to share your blessings and take the actions you need to take toward emotional, mental, and spiritual well-being. Determine the best diet for your body and implement healthy eating strategies. Diversify how you exercise and get a good night's sleep for optimal health. Decide to be strong and in great condition and then ask the Angel of Health to inspire you to achieve this intention.

Chakras

All chakras in balance on all levels—mentally, emotionally, spiritually, and physically.

Colors

Blue for inner peace. *Green* for abundance and health. *Orange* for ability and the motivation to exercise and move your body. *Red* for vim, vigor, vitality, and a strong foundation. *Yellow* for good digestive function and the ability to integrate life events.

Gemstones

Citrine for mental clarity, for ease in digestion, and to integrate everything going on around you and within you. *Garnet* to increase energy, stamina, and vitality. *Green aventurine* for health, wealth, and happiness. *Jade* for good fortune, love, health, and wellness. *Ruby* to align with your core inner strength.

Essential Oils

Eucalyptus to stimulate and uplift the mind and body. *Lavender* to balance the body's physical and mental functions. *Ravensara* to release emotional patterns and inner torment as well as ward off germs. *Sweet marjoram* to encourage healthy breathing and deep, healing sleep. *Tea tree* for rapid healing of infections.

Supportive Archangels

Archangel Ariel for general health and vitality. *Archangel Chamuel* for balanced and healthy relationships. *Archangel Michael* to remove fears, stress, phobias, and obsessions to live a healthy life. *Archangel Muriel* for balanced emotions. *Archangel Raphael* to help you maintain good health and provide healing when needed. *Archangel Thuriel* for the overall good health of animals and nature. *Archangel Zadkiel* to transform and transmute challenging situations with mercy and compassion.

Suggested Petition

Oh, Angel of Health! Please guide me in being aware of the actions I need to take every day to be healthy. Help me to think positively and feel gratitude for my life to boost my immune system. I want to eat properly and exercise regularly. Inspire me to eat the foods that are perfect for my body type. Show me ways to balance my work and my playtime so that I feel emotionally and mentally fulfilled. Inspire me to choose good habits to maintain a healthy weight, glowing skin, strong hair and nails, and overall well-being. Thank you!

Affirmations

I am healthy, whole, and complete. My body, mind, and emotions are in balance. It is easy for me to heal any issue that arises—physically, mentally, and emotionally. I have plenty of energy. I am vital and healthy. I enjoy overall well-being.

ANGEL OF
HELPFUL PEOPLE

*D*o I feel supported in my life? Do I surround myself with helpful and caring people, including friends, family, coworkers, and even strangers? Am I equipped to lend a hand to others?

Call on the Angel of Helpful People to assist you in being thoughtful to others and to invite thoughtful people into your life. Recognize the importance of being in service to others, open yourself to helping those who need help, and observe the natural reciprocity that brings that support back around to you when you need it. Ask the Angel of Helpful People to bring you to the right people and circumstances in all that you do. Believe in the kindness of strangers as well as the kindness of your inner circle. Allow yourself to be part of the community and show loving kindness to all. Invite this angel to align you with good contacts and a network of people who can make the right introductions to other supportive people. This angel brings forth the vibration of being at the right place, at the right time, with the right people.

Chakras

Heart chakra to be open to allow blessings, mentors, and a multitude of ways to receive support. *Navel chakra* to recognize and know that you have emotional support when needed. *Root chakra* to encourage the presence of caring friends and family on a core level. *Throat chakra* to activate Divine timing to connect you with the right people who can help you.

Colors

Brick red to ground your experiences and establish a strong foundation and network of friends and colleagues. *Brown* to connect with the supportive energy of Mother Earth. *Metallic silver* to find positive takeaways in every nook and cranny of your physical, mental, emotional, and spiritual world. *Pastel yellow* to activate feelings of worthiness and deservedness. *White* to attract heavenly help or even an earthly "angel investor" or benefactor.

Gemstones

Agate geode to maintain a loving vibe so that people want to help you and feel comfortable doing so. *Dumortierite* to attract supportive people. *Galena* to solidify healthy and mutually beneficial relationships. *Kunzite* to attract and appreciate loving, thoughtful people in all areas of life. *Pyrite* to move forward with calmness and serenity, knowing that assistance is always available. *Scolecite* to acknowledge and utilize the help of angels and beneficial invisible helpers. *Stromatolite* to attract ethical, loyal business colleagues.

Essential Oils

Allspice to express gratitude for your community's help and encouragement. *Orange* to be a supportive friend and allow caring friends to support you. *Rosemary* to deflect negativity and align you with loyal, authentic friends and colleagues. *Sweet marjoram* to see and embrace loyal and caring friends in your life.

Supportive Archangels

Archangel Chamuel to encourage healthy relationships. *Archangel Muriel* to maintain emotional balance so that you are comfortable receiving help and others are comfortable helping you. *Archangel Raphael* to draw helpful people into your life during a period of healing. *Archangel Sabrael* to deter jealousy and to prevent negative energy from interfering with your cooperative relationships.

Suggested Petition

Oh, Angel of Helpful People! Please assist me in being open to receiving supportive friends and family in my life. I am ready to surround myself with conscious and considerate people who provide me with encouragement and emotional help. Help me do the same for them. Reveal to me the benefactors and supporters of my life and remind me to express my gratitude to them and in general on a regular basis. Help orchestrate a collaboration between me and my colleagues, friends, and family in various areas of my life. Thank you!

Affirmations

Wherever I go and whatever I do, I encounter plenty of people who want to support me. I am blessed with caring friends and family. Strangers I meet during the course of my day often bring blessings. I magnetically attract peaceful and thoughtful people into my circle. My friends and family are supportive of me. They are happy for all the good in my life.

ANGEL OF
INNER KNOWING

*D*o I have a tendency to vacillate when making decisions, regardless of their importance? Is there anything in me that blocks me from living life fully? Do I doubt myself?

Call on the Angel of Inner Knowing when you are indecisive and feel like you can't make a decision. If you are constantly asking others for their opinions or seeking guidance other than from within your own consciousness, then it is time for you to seek out with the Angel of Inner Knowing to be your ally. This is the angel to help you tap into that part of yourself that knows what to do and what to believe. You do have the answers within yourself, you just need to know how to look for them. Of course, there are times when you may need to seek advice from outside of yourself, but the majority of the time, you are the only one who knows what is best for you. Ask the Angel of Inner Knowing to help you find the answers you need within yourself first.

Chakras

Crown chakra to remember to pray for inspiration from within yourself. *Navel chakra* to activate your ability to come up with creative solutions. *Solar plexus chakra* to have the self-confidence to make decisions. *Third eye chakra* to see your life clearly from all perspectives. *Throat chakra* to receive inspiration from the angels and actualize it with your words and actions.

Colors

Gold to remember to consciously activate the golden flecks of light in your energy field that are a conduit for information, knowledge, and wisdom. *Royal blue* to align with peaceful knowing and higher intelligence. *White* to connect with the blessing of being able to discern and recognize information that is available to all.

Gemstones

Indicolite, also known as *blue tourmaline*, to support better comprehension and single-pointed focus. *Iolite* to organize your thoughts and to improve your ability to communicate what you know. *Lapis lazuli* to access knowledge, wisdom, and information. *Sapphire* to clear away distortions, reveal the truth, and improve inner knowing. *Sodalite* to increase your intuition and open the channel for higher wisdom.

Essential Oils

Frankincense to align with higher consciousness and increase your awareness of the spiritual and mystical experience of the unity of the universe. *Grapefruit* to raise your vibration to receive messages from angels, archangels, and master teachers. *Sandalwood* to activate the wise scholar within.

Supportive Archangels

Archangel Gabriel to inspire and guide you through symbols and dreams. *Archangel Jophiel* to align you with the wisdom stored within you. *Archangel Metatron* to help you tap into higher states of consciousness and the records of all that is, all that was, and all potential future realities.

Suggested Petition

Oh, Angel of Inner Knowing! Please help me trust myself and know what I need to know when I need to know it. I often have trouble deciding between choices, whether it is a big decision like whether to say yes to a new opportunity or a small one such as what to eat or what to wear. Help me trust my inner knowing and show me how to improve my ability to believe in myself and make it easier for me to make decisions. Thank you!

Affirmations

I can see the unseen and hear the unsaid. I acknowledge and trust my intuition. It is my intention to improve my spiritual sight and clairvoyant capabilities. Hidden intentions, masks, and illusions are disclosed. I trust my own inner knowing. It is easy for me to make decisions.

ANGEL OF INNER PEACE

*I*s having inner peace at the forefront of my awareness? Do I take the actions necessary to cultivate inner peace? What can I do to find the center of peace within myself?

Call on the Angel of Inner Peace to help shift your awareness away from repetitive thoughts or incessant mind chatter to focus on thoughts that promote inner peace and emotional balance. The vibe of this angel can assist you in letting go and releasing situations in your past—both those that are recent as well as those that happened many years ago—and find inner peace and true happiness. By releasing old thoughts and situations that stand opposed to your mental, emotional, and spiritual well-being and actively cultivating inner peace, you invite positive situations and relationships into your life. Invite the Angel of Inner Peace to help you focus on the positives that come your way and to help you avoid escalating or overthinking the negatives so you can maintain your peace and balance going forward.

Chakras

Crown chakra to align with the Divine with a quiet mind. *Heart chakra* to focus on love and all that is good. *Navel chakra* for emotional balance. *Third eye chakra* to maintain a meditation practice for stress relief.

Colors

Light blue to invite restful and peaceful feelings. *Light pink* for comfort and compassion for yourself and others. *Seafoam green* to elicit the energy of the tranquil waters of comfort and warmth.

Gemstones

Dumortierite to enhance mental acuity and help you hear, sense, and know Divine information. *Hematite* to reduce hyperactivity. *Kambaba jasper* to allow more love, calm, and tolerance into your consciousness and to align with the inner peace inherent in your true nature. *Lapis lazuli* to heal emotional turmoil and find inner peace. *Magenta-dyed agate* to balance your emotions and increase your emotional maturity. *Malachite* to become consciously aware of repetitive patterns that are not for your highest good and to make the necessary adjustments to cultivate inner peace. *Ruby in zoisite* to amplify the vibration of love and comfort. *Scolecite* to adjust your behavior, attitude, and responses as you awaken your spiritual consciousness. *Selenite* to attain freedom from suffering and to tune into your intuitive gifts. *Sodalite* to be calm, relaxed, and stress-free. *Sugilite* to activate the transformative power of love.

Essential Oils

Angelica to calm the mind's incessant chatter. *Chamomile* to quiet your mind, quell emotional outbursts, heal frayed nerves, and cancel out angry or vindictive thoughts. *Clary sage* to calm aggressiveness and to lower tension and hyperactivity. *Frankincense* to align with compassion, inner peace, tolerance, and love. *Lavender* to experience tranquility and inner peace. *Lime* to release fears and perceived blocks and experience the sweetness of life. *Mandarin* to elicit feelings of safety and joy. *Sandalwood* to align you with compassion, inner peace, tolerance, and love. *Spikenard* to increase emotional maturity by calming and balancing your emotions. *Spruce* to transform anger and frustration and to cultivate tranquility. *Sweet marjoram* to reduce anxiety and release hysteria. *Ylang-ylang* for a calm and relaxed outlook on life.

Supportive Archangels

Archangel Auriel to release your subconscious fears. *Archangel Gabriel* for inspiration and guidance, dream interpretation, and inner knowing. *Arch-

angel Sabrael to release feelings of jealousy and patterns of thought that will eventually harm you. *Archangel Uriel* to increase the frequency of "aha" moments, those moments of expanded awareness where everything makes sense. *Archangel Zadkiel* for personal transformation and to enhance meditative practices that bring peaceful thoughts.

Suggested Petition

Oh, Angel of Inner Peace! Please help me let go of memories of life experiences that cause me angst. Show me the tools to help me reduce emotional, physical, and mental inflammation. I need help to visualize positive outcomes and to have faith and trust in life's experiences. Help me ease tension and show me how to temper my reactions. I want to release subconscious fears and be more emotionally mature and grounded. Motivate me to quiet my mind, take time for contemplation, and meditate to help get me to a place of inner peace. Thank you!

Affirmations

I easily transform anger and frustration into tranquility and inner peace through conscious release and awareness. I am calm. I am relaxed. All is well. I am aligned with the healing powers of inner peace and kindness. I am extremely intuitive. I am at peace with myself and the world around me.

ANGEL OF INNER STRENGTH

*D*o I know who I am? Am I willing to learn from my mistakes? Do I have the discipline and strong resolve to keep going forward, even when the going gets tough?

Call on the Angel of Inner Strength when you need to have the fortitude and resolve to make positive choices. This is the angel to petition when you need to call on your core strength and the courage to withstand adversity. This angel helps you find mental and emotional strength of character to withstand situations where you might feel intimidated or fearful so you can push through them. The Angel of Inner Strength can be a powerful ally as you develop your intellectual power and cultivate your resolve to remain steadfast in your actions and your positions. Call on your unique skills and capabilities to build your inner strength. The Angel of Inner Strength can help you stay positive, grounded, and centered within yourself so you can have integrity of character, maintain mental focus, and be unwavering in your purpose.

Chakras

Crown chakra to align with your highest potential and activate the miracle worker within you. *Root chakra* to stay grounded, focused, and strong. *Solar plexus chakra* to shine your light with confidence and strength.

Colors

Black to ward off psychic energy that may try to interfere with your highest purpose. *Gold* to encourage you to live life to your fullest potential. *Red* to activate your vitality and core strength. *Silver* to find the blessings in all situations and to recognize how to utilize them for the good of all. *White* to help you remember who you truly are. *Yellow* to feel confident and courageous to fulfill your soul's agreements.

Gemstones

Black tourmaline to deflect and remove negative forces from your energy field and physical space. *Citrine* to stay positive and overcome insecurities. *Garnet* to vitalize your passion and take grounded action. *Peridot* to transcend challenges and to recognize the unlimited possibilities in all situations. *Pyrite* to believe in yourself, access your courage, and pursue your dreams. *Red tiger's eye* to develop a strong foundation and to maintain focus on your core needs and core strength. *Rhodochrosite* to know that it is safe for you to be powerful. *Ruby* to improve your vital life force. *Rutilated quartz* to acquire the self-motivation to live life to the fullest. *Sapphire* to embrace a calmness of mind and a resolute spirit. *Selenite* to stay focused on your spiritual path and your personal spiritual truth. *Tiger iron* to stay grounded and to feel sure of yourself and your abilities.

Essential Oils

Benzoin to take thoughtful, focused action toward your chosen path. *Bergamot* to increase your confidence and mental clarity. *Peppermint* to propel you ahead in the direction you need to go. *Red thyme* to improve determination and to help you align with your soul's purpose. *Sweet marjoram* to shore up inner strength and courage when you are feeling emotionally weak and vulnerable.

Supportive Archangels

Archangel Chamuel to align with compassion and inner peace. *Archangel Haniel* to communicate with your higher self and to remember who you truly are. *Archangel Michael* to feel safe and to know that you are always divinely protected. *Archangel Muriel* to realign emotions, balance your awareness, and cultivate resolve.

Suggested Petition

Oh, Angel of Inner Strength! Please inspire me to cultivate the resolve to move in the direction I need to go. Help me when I am feeling vulnerable and emotionally out of balance. Show me how to embody the truth that the power of inner strength is greater than extreme disciplines and forced behaviors. Help me focus on my truth and forge forward with determination and joy. Show me ways to remember and know that I am safe and have great inner strength to overcome any of life's challenges. Thank you!

Affirmations

It is safe for me to be powerful in loving ways. I am magnificent! I have the strength to do anything I set out to do with loving intention. I am grateful for the courage to be all I can be. I have great inner strength. I'm grounded, focused, and tuned into the Universe. I stay on task with the projects at hand. My inner strength shines through in all I do.

ANGEL OF INTELLIGENCE

*D*o I need more mental clarity? Am I consciously aware of all my thoughts? What knowledge do I need to acquire, remember, or realize?

Call on the Angel of Intelligence when you need more brainpower. This angel can help you employ your powers of reasoning and comprehension to make intelligent decisions on a matter or project. Call on this angel when you are trying something new or learning something for the first time so that you can integrate that knowledge or skill and remember it for future use. This angel is your ally to increase your ability to acquire and retain knowledge and apply that information in a skillful way. Mental acuity allows you to properly gather and then utilize information to its greatest potential. The Angel of Intelligence can help you apply the knowledge you have to solve problems or create new things that help yourself and others. This angel is especially beneficial for the aging to bring mental agility and encourage memory recall.

Chakras

Crown chakra to remember your connection with higher knowledge and the Divine spark within. *Third eye chakra* to maintain a connection with your intuition and apply your realizations to your intellectual knowledge. *Throat chakra* to hear the answers to life's questions and to know how to proceed.

Colors

Cobalt blue to align with the higher wisdom and knowledge. *Navy blue* to spend time in contemplative thought. *Olive green* to embrace concepts that may seem far out at first glance. *Purple* to recognize aspects of yourself that were previously hidden behind old preconceived notions. *Silver* to tap into higher thought and wisdom. *White* to eliminate scattered thinking and fine-tune your thoughts.

Gemstones

Amethyst to activate the mind to receive and understand higher wisdom and knowledge. *Apophyllite* to focus your mind to sort through details for thorough integration and understanding of a given subject. *Bismuth* to remind yourself that you can improve your mental capacity by organizing your thoughts. *Clear quartz* for clarity and focus. *Fluorite*, known as the "genius stone," to align with Divine intelligence and enhance your ability to focus. *Hematite* to remove scattered energy from your energy field and to repel negative thoughts. *Herkimer diamond* to shine light on any subject and sharpen mental focus. *Labradorite* to find answers through inner and outer reflections. *Moldavite* to tap into concepts that are in the outer limits of your present awareness. *Selenite* to activate your connection with ancient wisdom and knowledge. *Zebra jasper* for mental clarity and to keep you focused on attainable goals.

Essential Oils

Bergamot for mental clarity, confidence, and a joyful outlook on life. *Black pepper* to speed up your thought processes and relieve sluggishness. *Grapefruit* to sharpen memory and mental clarity. *Mandarin* for mental clarity and a sharp mind. *Peppermint* to relieve mental fatigue, maintain alertness, and stimulate mental clarity and focus. *Rosemary* to encourage mental alertness and promote more presence in daily activities.

Supportive Archangels

Archangel Gabriel for inspiration and inner knowing and to receive and understand higher knowledge. *Archangel Metatron* to hear and know higher knowledge and wisdom. *Archangel Michael* to activate your mental capacity, intelligence, and swift action based on clear observations. *Archangel Sabrael* to ward off incessant mind chatter, which will improve meditation and contemplative thought.

Suggested Petition

Oh, Angel of Intelligence! I am trying to figure something out, and I need help gaining perspective. I want to access my memory and activate the neurons in my brain to create pathways for solutions and new ideas. Help me think outside the box and realize that there are many ways to discover new information or uncover previously known information that may be useful. Let me take the action to create the perfect space to align with my intellectual nature and to spend time with people who are intellectually adept. Thank you!

Affirmations

I am an intelligent being with the ability to focus on complex tasks. I enjoy learning new things and easily tap into my memory to retrieve information I've learned. I am clear, energized, and connected. I have great mental and emotional clarity. It is easy for me to awaken my consciousness and to be fully present in my daily activities. I am grounded and focused.

ANGEL OF INTUITION

*W*hy do I often know certain things about people or situations without a logical explanation? How can I develop self-trust to believe in myself? How can I discern if my intuition is leading me down the right path?

Call on the Angel of Intuition to improve your ability to recognize the signs and symbols that reveal the truth about a situation. This angel can awaken your awareness so that you are more apt to pay attention and notice these signs and interpret them properly. The Angel of Intuition is a great guide when you are learning to accept the fact that you are, in fact, intuitive. This angel can also help you believe yourself when you feel, sense, see, or know something that is beyond the ordinary explanation of what you "should" or "can" know. This angel can help you discern which thoughts and feelings are yours and which are stemming from the consciousness of others, and this angel can help you block out those thoughts and feelings that are unhelpful to the situation at hand.

Chakras

Crown chakra to connect with Divine consciousness through higher intuition. *Navel chakra* to experience gut feelings and take action based upon those feelings. *Solar plexus chakra* for the confidence and courage to trust your realizations and integrate them into your life. *Third eye chakra* for the ability to see the unseen, know the unknown, and hear what is not being said.

Colors

Indigo blue for intuition, knowing, and dreaming. *Pastel blue* to hear telepathic guidance. *White* to receive higher intuition.

Gemstones

Amethyst to keep your aura cleansed so that you can see, hear, know, and feel the truth through your innate intuition. *Ametrine* to help you feel safe and confident as you practice your extrasensory perception. *Angelite* to align with Divine timing, angelic communication, and spirit guide awareness. *Apophyllite* to channel and understand messages from the Universe with constant awareness. *Charoite* to clearly comprehend the details of everything around you and align with the cosmos. *Hiddenite* to improve intuitive insights and provide a buffer when you are extremely sensitive to the thoughts, feelings, physical challenges, and emotions of others. *Kyanite* to align your spiritual nature with higher realms of consciousness to enhance your ability to receive and transmit information on all levels. *Lapis lazuli* to improve your spiritual sight and meditation practice. *Magenta-dyed agate* to be receptive to your intuition and accept the part of you that sees and holds a vision for a better way of life for all beings. *Moonstone* for greater perspective and to amplify receptivity and awareness of life cycles. *Selenite* to activate your connection with your intuitive nature.

Essential Oils

Angelica to calm the mind's incessant chatter and provide a sense of serenity so that you can hear and know guidance from within. *Black pepper* to help you embrace your gifts of intuition and prophecy. *Elemi* to activate your intuition along with a sense of assuredness. *Melissa* to be open to receive messages and guidance while raising your confidence in your intuitive experience. *Sandalwood* to trust your awareness of your feelings and to aid in developing a spiritual practice. *Spikenard* to help highly intuitive people deal with incoming energies.

Supportive Archangels

Archangel Ariel to guide you to trust your intuitive realization and the courage to act upon that knowledge. *Archangel Gabriel* to open your spiritual ears and eyes to intuitive guidance. *Archangel Michael* to feel safe and sound as you develop and use your intuition. *Archangel Raziel* to instill confidence in your own inner knowing and the voice within. *Archangel Seraphiel* to reawaken your knowledge and connection with the angelic realm, which provides the insights and information required for intuitive realizations. *Archangel Uriel* to awaken your awareness of your spiritual purpose.

Suggested Petition

Oh, Angel of Intuition! Please help me develop my ability to understand or know something beyond the ordinary. Help me trust my intuitive hunches and believe myself when I feel like I know something even when it isn't obvious to others. Help me follow my gut and determine the perfect strategy or approach to personal situations. Let me see and interpret signs and symbols from the Divine and apply them. Open my ears to hear my inner voice and let that voice be clear and concise. I want to trust my feelings and do what is right for me and the highest good for all concerned. Thank you!

Affirmations

I am extremely intuitive. Divine messages are being sent to me all the time. It is easy for me to interpret the messages and guidance I receive. I know my own truth and trust my inner wisdom. I look within and know the answers. I trust my intuition and gut feelings. My life flows easily with grace because my intuition leads the way.

ANGEL OF JUSTICE

*A*m I fair-minded in all my interactions? Do I need to be more objective in how I perceive others and their situations? Are the judgments I make of myself and others fair, equal, and ethical?

Call on the Angel of Justice when you need to align with moral rightness and fairness. When you find yourself questioning the way you are handling a situation in your life, this angel can help you discern the most just course of action to take. The need for fairness is paramount in good decision-making, along with kindness. If you've noticed that you or those around you aren't acting with integrity, take time to contemplate the way you are perceiving the situation at hand and consider whether you are being objective enough. Consider if the position you've been taking is equitable to everyone involved. This angel can help you tell the truth, play by the rules, be aware of how your actions affect others, be responsible for your own mistakes, be open-minded, and never take advantage of others.

Chakras

Heart chakra to remember to look into your heart to know if you are being honest, fair, and just. *Third eye chakra* to engage your intuition to realize if the situation is in integrity or if something underhanded is at play. *Throat chakra* to align with the truth—your own truth as well as the truth of the situation.

Colors

Cobalt blue to amplify honesty, truthfulness, fairness, and integrity—to be "true blue." *Green* to bring peaceful realizations with honest interactions for all involved. *Turquoise* for impartiality in communication.

Gemstones

Amazonite to align with honesty and truth. *Ametrine* to discern when people are acting in integrity and assuring that justice is served when they are not. *Blue calcite* to communicate with kindness regardless of what needs to be said. *Black tourmaline* to attract trustworthy people into your life. *Chevron amethyst* to strive for personal excellence and to be impeccable with your word. *Dalmatian jasper* to help you surround yourself with reliable, trustworthy people. *Hematite* to imagine yourself enveloped in a cloak of loving protection to keep unethical vibes out. *Turquoise* to set boundaries with anyone who does not come from a place of genuineness and integrity. *Window quartz* to explore the inner sanctums of your consciousness to check in on your own level of fidelity and dependability.

Essential Oils

Anise seed to use the lessons of the past as positive stepping-stones to your future. *Elemi* to break free and detach from situations that aren't fair or just. *Eucalyptus* to rid yourself of untrustworthy people and situations. *Geranium* to align with accountability, integrity, and truth. *Lemon* to increase self-esteem and trust your discernment abilities. *Myrrh* to attract loving, authentic, and trustworthy relationships. *Orange* to encourage connections with people of integrity. *Rosemary* to ward off negative situations and to attract loyal, authentic friends and romantic relationships. *Sage* to weed out untrustworthy people.

Supportive Archangels

Archangel Michael to oversee fairness in all situations. *Archangel Sachiel* for good fortune and beneficial outcomes in legal matters. *Archangel Zadkiel* to support you during legal disputes.

Suggested Petition

Oh, Angel of Justice! Please help me become aware of how I can be fairer and more just in my dealings with myself and others. Give me the inner strength to forgive past injustices and to set boundaries with those who are not coming from a place of genuineness and integrity. Shine light on the truth and give me the courage to speak up with grace so that justice is served. Thank you!

Affirmations

I live my truth. I easily and honestly communicate what is on my mind. I am impeccable with my word. I stand up for myself, and I say what I need to say. I surround myself with people who easily speak their truth. I deal with people fairly. I am impartial in other people's drama, and I do not take sides without knowing all the facts.

ANGEL OF LOYALTY

*A*m I a loyal person? Do I surround myself with faithful people who are loving and supportive? Am I supportive of and true to others?

Call on the Angel of Loyalty when you are experiencing situations where you have been betrayed or when you are fearing betrayal. This angel will help you learn how to be loyal and how to experience true love by nurturing your connection to unconditional love. You attract people and situations based on the vibration you are putting out. Start with yourself and practice self-observation. This will help you cultivate loyalty to yourself and to others, which you must do before you can clearly observe that loyalty being returned to you by others. This angel also helps you recognize disloyalty in yourself and others and helps you make wise decisions about where to place your devotion. Instill a constant devotion to being faithful to those you care about. Know where your loyalties lie and be steadfast with where you put your attention and your energy.

Chakras

Heart chakra to be truehearted and show allegiance to a person or situation. *Solar plexus chakra* to have the courage and confidence to be steadfast in your faithfulness. *Third eye chakra* to feel devotion to someone with clear vision of the meaning of being true to them.

Colors

Deep blue to attract loyal friendships and authentic experiences. *Pastel blue* to communicate the truth in all interactions. *Yellow* to symbolize confidence and intelligence.

Gemstones

Amazonite to reveal the truth. *Angelite* to find support from heavenly helpers and to recognize false friends for what they are. *Blue calcite* to discern which people and situations are dependable and trustworthy. *Blue lace agate* to align with tried-and-true connections. *Celestite* to bring forth dedicated, devoted people in all areas of your life. *Citrine* to courageously set a boundary when you realize that someone is not being loyal to you. *Golden topaz* to shine light on your brilliance and to feel strong enough to command one's allegiance. *Green tourmaline* for luck, loyalty, and success. *Iolite* to know that you are worthy of having dedicated and true associations. *Lapis lazuli* to amplify protection for you, your home, your family, your business, and all that is important to you. *Sapphire* to attract wise colleagues who are steadfast and loyal. *Sodalite* to maintain a sense of calm, peace, and inner knowing about yourself and the world around you.

Essential Oils

Orange to increase spiritual fortitude and to support you when you need to set a boundary with someone who has been disloyal. *Oregano* to chase away negative thoughts and to reveal if paranoid feelings are, in fact, justified. *Palo santo* to reveal disloyal people and to release jealousy and negative forces. *Peppermint* to deflect jealous energy from those who aren't true to you. *Rose* to expand your sphere of love and your ability to cultivate loyal relationships. *Rosemary* to attract loyal and authentic friends and romantic relationships and to weed out those who are untrustworthy. *Sandalwood* to improve your faith and loyalty to yourself as well as others.

Supportive Archangels

Archangel Chamuel to send good energy to heal past relationships and dissolve any negative patterns in friendships. *Archangel Jophiel* for loyalty, love, and wisdom. *Archangel Metatron* to align with doing the right thing in any and all circumstances. *Archangel Sabrael* to deflect jealous vibes while attracting honest and devoted people and circumstances.

Suggested Petition

Oh, Angel of Loyalty! Please help me rid myself of disingenuous people and shift my energy so that I only attract loyal and dedicated friends, family, and colleagues. Show me how to know myself better and identify where in my life I might be lacking in faithfulness and devotion. Stop me from gossiping about others and help me understand how that behavior attracts people who would speak poorly about me. Please keep me free of traitors, false friendships, and bad business relationships. Thank you!

Affirmations

My actions are heart-centered and loyal to others. I love authentically and fully. I am grateful for my supportive and caring friends. I attract loyal people into my life. I am a loyal and faithful person to all those I am in relationship with—both professional and personal. I cultivate and maintain meaningful relationships in my life, and we all support each other.

ANGEL OF MARRIAGE

*A*m I cultivating my romantic relationship with trust, attention, time, patience, honesty, and respect? Do I feel ready for a healthy marital relationship? Am I committed to deepening my bond with my partner?

Call on the Angel of Marriage when you are ready to deepen your relationship with your spouse or partner. This angel can instill the vibration of blessings on your relationship, encouraging fidelity, openness, consideration, and patience. Invoke this angel to improve your listening skills and the depth of emotional caring you feel for one another. With this angel in your entourage, you will better equip yourself to do what it takes to have a lasting and healthy marriage. This angel supports good communication, commitment, kindness, acceptance, and love. If you want to find your perfect life partner, this angel is your ally for attracting the right person who is willing to build a long-lasting marriage with you. This angel can help you discern if your current partner is meant to take that step into marriage with you and how to take the next steps toward that life change.

Chakras

Crown chakra to always remember to keep a place in your union for the Divine. *Heart chakra* to always have an intimate, loving connection with your spouse. *Navel chakra* to maintain balanced emotions and to cultivate your sensual connection. *Root chakra* for grounded connection and healthy sexual relations. *Solar plexus chakra* for self-confidence and the ability to establish healthy boundaries. *Third eye chakra* for good mind-to-mind communication and the ability to know your spouse on a deeper, higher level. *Throat chakra* for good communication and excellent listening skills.

Colors

Blue to be true to each other. *Forest green* to deepen your marital connection. *Light green* to stay heart-centered and focused on the loving energy between you and your partner. *Magenta* for a deeper, more intimate soul connection. *Pink* to provide emotional support and take nurturing actions. *Red* for great sex and sensual experiences with your partner.

Gemstones

Cobaltoan calcite to activate compassion, wisdom, tolerance, and kindness for the ultimate connection to unconditional love, mercy, and understanding. *Danburite* to invite harmony and cooperation into your marriage. *Hiddenite* to magnetically attract romance, love, and commitment. *Kunzite* to radiate love in all that you are and all that you do. *Magenta-dyed agate* to align your consciousness with compassion, nurturing energy, and great wisdom. *Rose quartz* to connect with your heart chakra, the center of your consciousness. *Unakite* to foster a healthy and happy relationship though balanced emotions.

Essential Oils

Allspice to amplify supportive energy and loyalty. *Patchouli* for passion and as an aphrodisiac. *Rose* symbolize a happy marriage. *Rosemary* for the vibration of loyalty and everlasting love. *Sweet marjoram* for loyalty and fidelity. *Ylang-ylang* to open your heart to soul-to-soul sexual connection.

Supportive Archangels

Archangel Chamuel to heal hurtful experiences in past romantic relationships and guide you toward your perfect lifelong partner. *Archangel Michael* to ensure a loyal and dedicated marriage. *Archangel Raphael* to heal your heart, mind, and emotions from any negative past romantic relationships.

Suggested Petition

If you are married:

Oh, Angel of Marriage! I am calling on you to bring the energies of the Divine into my relationship with my spouse. Please join with us to improve every aspect of our marriage. Help us to be kind and thoughtful to each other. Guide us to be the best marital partner we can be to and for each other. Surround us with the energy of true love, devotion, and dedication and bless our union. Help me to change my mindset to think as "we" rather than "me" to renew love in my life. Thank you!

If you want a marital partner:

Oh, Angel of Marriage! Please bring me my spouse. Please orchestrate the circumstances to let us meet and connect. Helps us to recognize each other on a soul level so we can develop and cultivate a good partnership for life-long companionship. Show me the way and show my future spouse the way so we can find each other and start our life together. Help me cultivate and nurture the loving relationships that are presently in my life and to attract more love into my life. Thank you!

Affirmations

I emanate harmony and love. I am grateful for my fantastic significant other, presently known or unknown. I allow love to envelop me. I have the best, most supportive spouse! I am so happy that my life partner is an everyday part off my life and brings to our union a sense of safety, support, and companionship, now and forever.

ANGEL OF MEDITATION AND CONTEMPLATION

*H*ow can I quiet my mind? What thoughts are predominant in my consciousness? Is there a way to slow down my thought processes?

Call on the Angel of Meditation and Contemplation when you need to reduce the amount of mental chatter going around and around in your mind. This angel assists with mindful presence and the ability to focus on one thing at a time, as well as helping you practice creating a space of no thoughts. Introspection is beneficial because it lets you observe and examine the thoughts that are in the forefront of your awareness so that you can align with your spiritual nature and awaken your awareness of the mystical aspects of your connection with the Divine. Ask this angel to help you move into deep, reflective thought without judgment. Move from contemplation into meditation by quieting your thoughts for periods of time—even for just seconds or minutes at a time. The practice of silencing your thoughts reduces stress, promotes well-being, and enhances self-awareness.

Chakras

Crown chakra to align you with tranquility and peace. *Heart chakra* to aid in focusing on love and inner peace. *Root chakra* to stay focused during contemplative thought. *Third eye chakra* to awaken your spiritual eyes and ability to see the unseen within yourself. *Throat chakra* to regulate the awareness of the practice of breathwork during meditation practices.

Colors

Black for grounded awareness. *Green* for heart-focused awareness. *Indigo blue* to align with deep contemplation. *Pastel blue* for peaceful awareness of the breath. *Pink* for loving awareness. *Purple* to connect with mystical and transformational realizations. *White* for purity in consciousness.

Gemstones

Ammonite to spiral deep within your mind for clarity and awareness. *Amethyst* to transform and transmute challenging thoughts and emotions that come up during meditation and contemplation. *Apophyllite* to sharpen inner focus and light the path to spiritual awareness. *Clear quartz* for mental clarity and spiritual connection. *Labradorite* for inner reflection. *Rose quartz* for self-love. *Smoky quartz* to stay grounded during the spiritual practice and dissolve unsettling emotions. *Selenite* to aid in contemplative thought.

Essential Oils

Bergamot to promote ease and to release feelings of anxiousness and symptoms of depression. *Frankincense* to align yourself with compassion, higher consciousness, inner peace, tolerance, and love. *Palmarosa* to clear your energetic space. *Sandalwood* to elicit a quiet mind, improve your confidence in spiritual pursuits, and align your mind and your heart with the Divine. *Sweet marjoram* to reduce inner turmoil and uncontrollable emotions.

Supportive Archangels

Archangel Gabriel to inspire and guide you in the dreamtime toward inner knowing. *Archangel Haniel* to lead you to an understanding of your soul's purpose. *Archangel Melchizedek* to aid you on your spiritual journey here on Earth and align you with your inner mystic. *Archangel Metatron* to start the process of reaching states of higher consciousness and enlightenment. *Archangel Muriel* to watch over you as you balance your emotions. *Archangel Raziel* to assist you as you awaken your innate spiritual gifts of clairvoyance, prophecy, revelation, and connection with the Great Mystery. *Archangel Uriel* to shine light on ideas and to awaken consciousness. *Archangel Zaphkiel* to deepen your understanding and mindfulness.

Suggested Petition

Oh, Angel of Meditation and Contemplation! Please watch over me and support me as I clear away the confusion of the mental chatter in my mind and emotions. Help me to sort through the layers of my awareness with nonjudgment and compassion. Aid in the release of extraneous thoughts and rid me of the negative emotions in my vibrational field. Show me how to let go of hurt feelings, injustices, and challenging feelings so I can improve my health and well-being and become a better person. Quiet my mind. Thank you!

Affirmations

I am aligned with the healing powers of inner peace and kindness. I am clearheaded and aligned with my natural rhythms. Meditation is effortless for me, and I practice regularly. I am thankful to be at peace. I am safe and sound. Divine protection always surrounds me. I am aligned and connected with this present moment.

ANGEL OF MENTAL STRENGTH

*W*hy do I feel like I can't accomplish my goals and dreams? Am I a good leader? Do I have the passion to make a difference? Can I regulate my thoughts and emotions and behave appropriately even when things get tough? Have I established goals?

Call on the Angel of Mental Strength when life seems harder than normal. This angel can aid you in overcoming the limiting thoughts and beliefs that are holding you back. Invite this angel to help you identify and replace negative thoughts and enhance mindfulness as you navigate challenges. Recognize that discomfort is temporary and that you can deal with any problem that arises. Exercise your mind by becoming self-aware and acknowledging your emotions. Establish goals and set yourself up for success by cultivating self-confidence, focus, and concentration. Decide to amplify self-control, positive energy, and determination. You can extend your efforts further by inviting the Angel of Determination and the Angel of Discipline to be a part of your heavenly entourage to improve your mental toughness and increase positive self-talk. You can also ask the Angel of Gratitude, the Angel of Meditation and Contemplation, and the Angel of Creative Intelligence to support you to improve your mental strength.

Chakras

Crown chakra for connection to higher thoughts and to your imagination. *Heart chakra* to maintain a state of gratitude. *Navel chakra* to find creative approaches to situations and to stay emotionally balanced. *Root chakra* to feel grounded, safe, and secure. *Solar plexus chakra* to cultivate self-confidence. *Third eye chakra* to improve mindfulness and the ability to hold a vision of the positive outcome.

Colors

Dark blue to examine the situation, find solutions, and take responsibility for your actions. *Metallic gray* to be steadfast and stay the course. *Pink* to remember how to comfort yourself when you are uncomfortable. *White* to think clearly and to find logic in your decision-making process. *Yellow* to encourage mental clarity and to think positive thoughts.

Gemstones

Black onyx to provide mental focus and grounding and the ability to stay on task. *Clear quartz* to stay focused and maintain clear thinking. *Fluorite* to support the brain in thinking through complex problems. *Petalite* to maintain a calm and balanced state of mental consciousness and to keep your perspective on reality. *Prasiolite* to enhance your mental strength and perseverance and to improve your focus and follow-through. *Pyrite* to offer a strong foundation to improve some of your core beliefs about yourself. *Tourmalinated quartz* to clear negative mental energy associated with jealousy, negative self-talk, confusing mental chatter, and general chaos.

Essential Oils

Basil to improve memory and to strengthen your ability to be successful. *Geranium* to attract safety and emotional balance. *Lemon* for confidence and clarity. *Rosemary* to improve your memory and ward off outside influences.

Supportive Archangels

Archangel Ariel for the general health of your mind and mental states. *Archangel Gabriel* to awaken your awareness to otherworldly information and insights. *Archangel Metatron* to encourage you to record the wisdom you receive and reframe the information so that it applies to everyday living. *Archangel Michael* for strength and courage on all levels. *Archangel Uriel* to light your path to higher states of consciousness as your soul evolves.

Suggested Petition

Oh, Angel of Mental Strength! I am asking for your help because I have been feeling a little scattered and dull, and I must stay focused on the completion of tasks. I know that I am intelligent, but I still need assistance to finish this project or to see this situation through to the end. Please activate the mental strength I need to accomplish whatever I put my mind to. Shine light on the steps to follow to ensure I have the necessary mental stamina to reach this goal. Thank you!

Affirmations

I am an intelligent being with the ability to focus on complex tasks. I am strong in body, mind, and soul. I am self-confident, determined, and capable. I can do anything I set out to do. Illusions fall away in front of me. I see through appearances and trust my intelligence without hesitation.

ANGEL OF NURTURING

*W*hat do I need to nurture in myself, in my life, and in others? Do I need to be more caring to other people in my life? Am I in need of support and encouragement?

Call on the Angel of Nurturing when you need to take better care of yourself or those around you. The process of caring for and encouraging well-being on all levels—mental, emotional, physical, and spiritual—is something that everyone needs. This includes the care of plants and animals in your life, as well as the people. This angel can help you give care and attention to your own personal development. Start with yourself and fill up your own cup first. You cannot pour out your nurturing to others if you are not properly nurtured yourself. When that cup is full, observe if you are giving plenty of attention to your parents, spouse, children, animals, garden, home, coworkers, and your business or workplace. Take good care of yourself and notice how this makes you a natural at caring for others.

Chakras

Heart chakra to focus on comfort and mercy. *Root chakra* to be grounded and know that all your needs are met with plenty of comfort tools available if you need extra care. *Solar plexus chakra* to relax and release stress or tension that might be preventing you from feeling nurtured and safe.

Colors

Pink to align with nurturing energy available from many sources. *Seafoam green* to elicit the energy of the tranquil waters of comfort and warmth.

Gemstones

Chrysocolla to calm anger, frustration, and feelings of unworthiness while promoting healing and inner peace. *Chrysoprase* to heighten compassion for yourself and to encourage feelings of self-love and confidence. *Cobra jasper* to align with the nurturing vibrations of nature. *Green calcite* for when you are having a change of heart and need time to adjust and nurture yourself as change takes place. *Kunzite* to relieve feelings of depression and anxiety and to help you understand how you want to be loved and how to love yourself. *Morganite* to help you take time to nurture yourself and feel love and happiness. *Phosphosiderite* to heal sorrow from past hurts and emotional wounds as you step into grace and hope. *Pink calcite* to attract loving relationships and to cultivate your existing relationships with all life—people, animals, and nature alike. *Pink tourmaline* to connect with unconditional love and your own loving vibrations, thoughts, and feelings. *Prehnite* to be receptive to great happiness in your life as a normal, everyday occurrence. *Rose quartz* to remember that you *are* love and to feel love. *Unakite* to balance yourself by engaging in self-nurturing activities and releasing distorted emotions and personal bias. *Watermelon tourmaline* for self-acceptance and to recognize that you are love at your core.

Essential Oils

Clary sage to help relax the drive to overachieve. *Frankincense* to restore youthfulness, health, and strength. *Geranium* to regenerate and rejuvenate your energy on all levels. *Ginger* to rejuvenate your body. *Lavender* to attract or renew more love into your life. *Rosewood* to stimulate healing and encourage feelings of well-being during rehabilitation. *Spruce* to feel rejuvenated by the vibration of this evergreen tree. *Sweet marjoram* to cultivate and nurture the loyal and loving relationships that you presently enjoy.

Supportive Archangels

Archangel Ariel to promote overall health and encourage rejuvenating activities. *Archangel Jophiel* to encourage self-love, beauty, and comfort. *Archangel Muriel* to support you while you nurture your emotional body. *Archangel Raphael* to inspire rest, restore, and rejuvenate on all levels.

Suggested Petition

Oh, Angel of Nurturing! Please help me practice self-care and allow love into my life. Inspire me with all the ways I can give myself the care and attention I need to feel good about myself. Then show me the ways to share my loving attention with others and cultivate well-being for all. I want to care for myself, encourage personal development, and rid myself of unwelcome thoughts and feelings. Let me foster feelings of loving kindness in all my thoughts, words, and actions. Thank you!

Affirmations

I am cared for, loved, and appreciated. Today I take good care of myself. I honor my body and my sacred space. I love myself. I love my body. I easily nurture myself. I know what to do to make myself feel better. I attract nurturing people into my life. I am nurtured and protected by the Divine.

ANGEL OF OPPORTUNITY

*A*m I embracing all the opportunities presented to me? Do I recognize opportunities when they arise? Have I hesitated when a set of circumstances made it possible for me to improve my life?

Call on the Angel of Opportunity when you would like favorable circumstances to present themselves. This angel is a wonderful ally during times of your life when you feel like you really need an opening or a lucky break. Ask this angel to improve your confidence when you are acting on ideas for advancement or success. This angel can keep you from hesitating when a window of opportunity opens. Opportunities often come with an expiration date, so timing your response accordingly is essential; hesitation is not recommended. This angel helps you embrace the idea that taking an action toward an opportunity, even if that action doesn't initially appear to make a difference, is better than taking no action at all. You will never know how much positive potential an opportunity brings until you try, and this angel supports you in acting upon and embracing your opportunities.

Chakras

Crown chakra to pay attention to Divine inspiration and gain clear direction. *Navel chakra* to give you the courage and energy to take action. *Root chakra* to feel the strength of your foundation upon which you can build further success. *Solar plexus chakra* to be sure of yourself and to use your high self-esteem to act upon realizations and ideas. *Third eye chakra* to remember dreams or the main message from dreamtime activities so that you can put them into reality.

Colors

Orange to feel brave and courageous so that there is no hesitation—only action. *Red* to passionately embrace the opportunities presented. *White* for inspired thought and higher realizations.

Gemstones

Carnelian to act upon creative ideas without hesitation. *Chevron amethyst* to develop your intuition and prophetic dreaming. *Golden topaz* to create new pathways of consciousness by experiencing unexplored avenues. *Green aventurine* to have the best luck and good fortune, thereby attracting favorable opportunities. *Green tourmaline* to have the acumen to recognize a blessed opening for good fortune. *Moldavite* to recognize out-of-this-world chances and opportunities. *Tektite* to open your spiritual sight to realize favorable, future-potential realities. *Vanadinite* to connect with the opportunity to channel inspired works—from musical compositions to technological gadgets.

Essential Oils

Basil to untangle chaotic thoughts and shed light on confusing circumstances and complex situations. *Clove* to imagine a positive outcome for a circumstance that requires strength.

Supportive Archangels

Archangel Haniel to tap into your soul's purpose as it relates to opportunities. *Archangel Jophiel* to trust your inner wisdom. *Archangel Metatron* to open your consciousness to recognize opportunities on a deep, all-knowing level. *Archangel Sachiel* for managing great success, extraordinary wealth, and prosperity. *Archangel Uriel* for creative thoughts and ideas and alignment with the universal flow.

Suggested Petition

Oh, Angel of Opportunity! Please open my eyes, my ears, my heart, and my mind to notice and recognize when an opportunity presents itself. Deliver dreams and inspired thoughts into my awareness and make sure I get the message. Help me to be brave enough to jump into action with my ideas. Prevent me from hesitating out of fear or subconscious sabotage. Show me how to walk through the door of opportunity for the highest good of all concerned. I am willing to receive unexpected blessings. I will continue to strive to improve myself so that I am well equipped to act upon opportunities as they show up. Thank you!

Affirmations

I see life from a higher perspective, which allows me to recognize favorable opportunities in my vast field of awareness. There are plenty of opportunities that match my talents. I am grateful that doors open to allow my dreams to come true. I seize opportunities with gratitude and a positive attitude.

ANGEL OF ORDER AND ORGANIZATION

*A*m I caught up in illusions and confusion? Is my home, car, closet, or any one of my other spaces disorganized or cluttered? Do I feel chaotic and frenzied?

Call on the Angel of Order and Organization when you need to improve your ability to sort through the priorities in your life. Invite this angel to inspire you to establish a place for everything and to keep everything in its place. This angel can be a powerful ally to help you clear out chaos and clutter and focus on details, scheduling, or anything that requires organization. Ask for the help you need to remove the extraneous from your life and shine light on ideas and information that will benefit you and others. The vibe that the Angel of Order and Organization brings can help you figure out what should stay and what should go—in any and all parts of your life. Use this vibration to stay strong and to align yourself with the ability to see things clearly.

Chakras

Crown chakra to have a clear connection to higher wisdom and knowledge. *Root chakra* to be focused and grounded enough to take the action to clear out anything that is unnecessary. *Solar plexus chakra* to have the confidence to take on the job of clearing out people, situations, and stuff that prevent you from shining your light fully. *Third eye chakra* to see your life clearly and from a higher perspective.

Colors

Black to have the contrast necessary to see order. *White* to align with the bright energy of things that are clean and clear. *Yellow* to remind you that your path to the future is free of obstacles.

Gemstones

Aragonite to locate your center and to direct you forward in a clear and concise manner to find creative solutions. *Bismuth* to approach things one step at a time in an organized, methodical manner. *Clear quartz laser wand* to sharpen your ability to stay focused and to have a systematic approach to organizing things. *Dumortierite* to hear, sense, and know direction that brings order, peace, and tranquility. *Fluorite* to use your intelligence to think through the best way to put things in order. *Malachite* to help you visualize clearing away unhealthy repetitive patterns. *Optical calcite* to see things clearly and to make sense of what is before you. *Petrified wood* to assist you in the process of clearing out any clutter that no longer serves you. *Prasiolite* to improve your ability to stay focused and to bring a task to completion. *Trilobite* to determine the order in which things need to take place for optimal productivity. *Zebra jasper* to sort through and see all the details, even when things aren't black and white.

Essential Oils

Bergamot to sort out the details of what's going on around you and within you. *Black pepper* to courageously clear away blocks, clutter, and disarray to be more able to fulfill your life agreements. *Cardamom* for dealing with details, scheduling, and organizing. *Fennel* to employ a grounded approach to gather realistic solutions to the challenge of organizing. *Lavender* to clear and calm the mind and to help you sort out the details and release chaos. *Lemon* for mental clarity so that you can focus your attention on the work required.

Supportive Archangels

Archangel Ariel for the energy and strength to sort through potentially messy situations or places. *Archangel Haniel* to connect with the truth through observation and order. *Archangel Michael* to cut the cords of attachment to disarray and items that are no longer needed. *Archangel Raphael* to heal attachments to things that are no longer for your highest good. *Archangel Uriel* to develop a better understanding of your responsibilities.

Suggested Petition

Oh, Angel of Order and Organization! Please help me see the mess and disarray in my world and motive me to do something about it. I want to release the mayhem and confusion that is caused by disorganization and excess around me. Inspire me to take action to release unnecessary objects, people, and situations. Give me ideas and visions to help me visualize a better way to arrange my life—my physical belongings as well as my thoughts and emotions. Thank you!

Affirmations

I am organized. I am prepared. Fine-pointed clarity is mine. It is easy for me to organize and bring order out of what appears to be chaos. My creative mind easily comes up with solutions for clearing out what is unnecessary. Arranging my space and my life in an organized manner creates ease and flow. It is with clear intentions that I move forward, self-assured and confident.

ANGEL OF PARTNERSHIP

*A*m I willing to enter into a business partnership for a common goal? Am I better off doing things alone or do I want to collaborate with someone regularly? How good am I at sharing in the business decisions, as well as the risks and potential profits?

Call on the Angel of Partnership when you are facing the decision to engage in a business partnership. Ask this angel to help you be open to sharing the management, profits, and responsibilities involved in running a business. The Angel of Partnership is good to have on your team to assure that you are doing your part in the business and to help you ensure that your partner is holding up their end of the deal. The vibe of this angel will help you establish and clearly define your business goals and objectives so every member of your team is aware of their defined purpose and their job responsibilities. Become part of the best team you possibly can and strategically plan all aspects of your business partnership, from costs and labor to publicity and marketing, so that you can achieve success in all areas of your business.

Chakras

All chakras to be totally present on all levels.

Colors

Black to know that your partnership is divinely protected. *Blue* to ensure good communication skills. *Orange* for the impetus to take action and get things done. *Red* for endurance, passion, and vitality. *Yellow* to attract the vibration of golden opportunities.

Gemstones

Black tourmaline to amplify your grounded determination and strong foundation. *Carnelian* to be proactive and self-motivated as you play your role in the partnership. *Citrine* to increase clarity and conviction to move through perceived blocks and be the best partner you can be. *Fire agate* to shift your entrepreneurial ideas into a determined drive to succeed. *Green tourmaline* for determination and passion to succeed while remaining heart centered. *Iolite* to promote longevity in your partnership. *Lapis lazuli* to maintain even-keeled and patient in your business dealings. *Sapphire* for a loyal and committed partnership. *Tanzanite* to improve confident communication. *Twin quartz crystal* to focus on the positive qualities you want to foster in your partnership.

Essential Oils

Allspice to cultivate the depth of friendship that goes along with a healthy partnership. *Basil* to attract the right partners. *Bay* to bring forth success and financial prosperity. *Bergamot* to maintain a strong sense of self and high self-esteem. *Black pepper* to cocreate a healthy and productive partnership. *Clove* to invite beneficial partnerships and financial success. *Sweet marjoram* to release negative emotions and maintain peaceful interactions.

Supportive Archangels

Archangel Jophiel for good relations with your partner. *Archangel Michael* to protect you from outside influences that might try to disrupt your good partnership. *Archangel Raziel* to support telepathic communication between you and your partner.

Suggested Petition

Oh, Angel of Partnership! Please help my partner and me realize our goals and objectives. Help us hold the vision and use our imagination to easily create a positive outcome. Help me to be fair and loyal to my partner, and vice versa. Shine light on our finances and business decisions so we make the best choices for the highest good of all involved. Inspire us to collaborate well together. Support both of us so we have the strength and endurance to overcome any challenges we might experience. Thank you!

Affirmations

I step forward in life with confidence and purpose. I have mental acuity regarding business partnerships. I have the courage to set boundaries with love and grace. I am protected from negative energy. Experiences from the past empower me. My partner and I collaborate on business matters with great success.

ANGEL OF PERSPECTIVE

*W*hat can I do to expand my perspective so that I don't miss anything? How can I embrace concepts that may seem far out at first glance? Am I listening to my inner guidance?

The Angel of Perspective helps you explore beyond the outer limits of your own core belief systems. With the guidance of this angel, you have the support to tap into another level of understanding and to see things from a much greater perspective. Imagine yourself rising high above life situations to gain a greater view. Use the Angel of Perspective as a guide to help you take the time for contemplative thought and inner reflection to gain understanding. Abstract thinking reveals new patterns and different perspectives to help you come up with creative solutions and ways to look at things differently. Ask this angel to create new pathways of consciousness by opening up unexplored avenues for raising your awareness. With the Angel of Perspective as your ally, you can bounce ideas off others to come up with innovative approaches to whatever task is at hand in both your personal and professional life.

Chakras

Heart chakra to sense, through your heart, various ways of seeing and feeling situations. *Navel chakra* to realize creative solutions on a gut level and to trust your feelings. *Root chakra* to stay grounded in your approach to various situations. *Solar plexus chakra* to brighten your mental outlook. *Third eye chakra* to use your intuition and to remember how to look at life and situations from various angles to truly grasp all that is going on.

Colors

Magenta to shift your awareness to a higher level to see things from a different angle. *Peach* to perceive the nuances of situations and the various "shades" of situations. *Purple* to connect with the power of transformation that is available when you use perspective. *Teal* to create a level of communication that exceeds the ordinary.

Gemstones

Botswana agate to recognize patterns and activate conscious awareness. *Dolomite* to improve your meditation experience and to create new pathways of consciousness. *Dumortierite* to see life from a higher perspective by activating your third eye chakra. *Golden calcite* to improve your situational awareness (the awareness of the elements in your space and what is happening around you). *Green moss agate* to remember to hold thoughts and concepts to the light to reveal the inner workings of situations. *Howlite* to shed light on emotional stress and to relieve pressure on potentially explosive situations. *Indochinite tektite*, a natural meteoric glass, to activate your intuition and to discover the unlimited potential of your spiritual growth into as-yet-unexplored dimensions. *Labradorite* to reflect and observe how the world around you mirrors the world within you. *Lepidolite* to tap into a higher level of understanding. *Moldavite* to expand your mind to think beyond the ordinary. *Moonstone* for greater perspective and to amplify receptivity and awareness of life cycles. *Zebra jasper* to read between the lines and see life from various angles.

Essential Oils

Black pepper to define and sharpen your intelligence and powers of observation. *Elemi* to bring peaceful realizations that help you see the truth and the bigger picture. *Eucalyptus* to clear out toxic thoughts and painful emotions to allow for greater clarity, as if you have foresight. *Grapefruit* to gain clarity and to have a clearer picture of what is truly going on within you and around you. *Lemon* to become aware of repetitive patterns of self-limiting thoughts that could be holding you back from observing the bigger picture. *Mandarin* to improve observation and sharpen your mind. *Rosemary* for mental clarity, memory improvement, and to shift how you think about yourself.

Supportive Archangels

Archangel Gabriel for inspiration, guidance, and dreamtime insights. *Archangel Metatron* for new realizations and to bring awareness to your soul's evolutionary process. *Archangel Michael* to see life from a higher and greater perspective.

Suggested Petition

Oh, Angel of Perspective! Please help me quiet my mind long enough to contemplate and reflect. Shine light on my ability to perceive life through a wide-angle lens. Open my awareness to better see my relationship with myself and others. Help reveal previously hidden aspects of myself and characteristics that were eclipsed behind old preconceived notions. Help me grasp the greater reality and touch upon increased self-knowledge as well as tolerance for others. Thank you!

Affirmations

Blessings come into my life seemingly from out of nowhere. I have unlimited potential and my possibilities are endless. I am very perceptive and discerning in all areas of my life. I see things from varying perspectives. My intuition is strong. I perceive life from a higher perspective. I take time for reflection. I observe how the world around me is a mirror of the world within me.

ANGEL OF PHYSICAL STRENGTH

*D*o I feel physically strong? Do I exercise regularly to tone and strengthen my core muscles? Do I feel healthy and fit in my body?

Call on the Angel of Physical Strength when you feel your endurance is lacking and that you tire easily. With this angel by your side, you can find the motivation you need to take the action required to strengthen your core and improve your physical endurance. Ask this angel to guide you to the right activities for your body type to improve your physical structure. Check in with your body frequently and learn to recognize any signs that you need to change your diet, whether by adding certain foods or eliminating certain foods, to support your intention to strengthen your body. Make a commitment to exercise regularly, diversifying your activities, and remain steadfast in your decision. Be mindful of the good feelings that come along with physical exercise and look forward to feeling good about being inside your body.

Chakras

Navel chakra to connect with your place of power and inner strength. *Root chakra* to stay grounded and focused and to connect with your vital life force. *Solar plexus chakra* for optimum digestive function to properly process nutrients to support strengthening activities.

Colors

Black to be grounded and rooted in your perceptions of reality. *Red* to connect with inner power, strength, vim, vigor, and endurance. *White* for higher and clearer perspectives.

Gemstones

Chalcopyrite to enhance the benefits of muscle-building exercises. *Orange calcite* to support a healthy spine and to ease muscular tension. *Prasiolite* to ward off germs and viruses and to rebalance yourself when dealing with health challenges. *Pyrite* for physical protection and a strong foundation. *Ruby* to increase vital life force and endurance. *Rutilated quartz* to improve energy levels and endurance for a strong body. *Selenite* to strengthen your core physical structure. *Septarian* to strengthen bones and relieve stressed muscles.

Essential Oils

Allspice to recognize your strength. *Cinnamon* to strengthen your heart. *Coriander* to promote new growth and to restore your overall structure. *Frankincense* to restore youthfulness. *Geranium* to improve health. *Grapefruit* to improve digestion and to renew health and strength. *Lemongrass* for muscle suppleness.

Supportive Archangels

Archangel Ariel for general health and vitality. *Archangel Chamael* to connect with well-balanced masculine energy. *Archangel Raphael* for a healthy physical body.

Suggested Petition

Oh, Angel of Physical Strength! Please guide me to maintain an energized, healthy, and strong body. Please help me connect with the vital life force that flows vibrantly through me. Increase my general health and guide me to take the action necessary to feel vital and fit. Connect me with feelings of passion so I can live life with vim and vigor. Show me how to be vibrant and strong. Inspire me to move my body and increase endurance. Thank you!

Affirmations

My energy is balanced. My physical structure is strong. I get sufficient sunlight to maintain a healthy body. I move my body and exercise regularly. My physical vitality and endurance are increasing. My body is rock solid. I focus on my intentions and take positive action to manifest my goals. I am grateful that my vital life force provides me with the energy and motivation to live life to the fullest.

ANGEL OF PROTECTION

*W*hy don't I feel safe? Who or what do I need to be protected from? Are there situations or relationships in my life that make me feel afraid?

Call on the Angel of Protection when your life feels out of control or you feel unsafe. You may need protection from your own thoughts and emotions first! Ask this angel to help you become conscious of how you attract situations that require you to need protection. This angel can help protect you from outside influences as well. If you are feeling unsafe, start with yourself and pray. Pray that you can clear your mind, heart, and emotions of fear, and pray that you will be divinely protected by legions of angels. Use your imagination to envision yourself surrounded by an entourage of angels who deflect the negative thoughts, feelings, energies, and actions that come from others. Ask the Angel of Protection to create a shield of shimmering white light around you that transforms and transmutes anything in your space that isn't love into love.

Chakras

Crown chakra to align with the highest level of Divine protection. *Navel chakra* to connect with your gut feelings. *Root chakra* to stay focused and grounded. *Solar plexus chakra* to have the confidence to shine brightly. *Third eye chakra* to follow your instincts and pay attention to what's going on around you.

Colors

Black to deflect negative energy. *Brown* to stay grounded. *Iridescent white* to amplify love swirling in your energy field. *Metallic gray* to expand the strong, safe energy field around you. *Pink* to amplify love and replace challenges. *Purple* to transform and transmute challenging situations.

Gemstones

Amethyst to transform and transmute challenging situations. *Black obsidian* to observe how the world around you is a reflection of your own inner mind and emotions. *Black tourmaline* to detract and deflect negative forces. *Galena* to ward off psychic attacks and to act as a constant reminder to maintain a protective sacred energy around you at all times. *Jet* to filter out energies that aren't for your highest good. *Lapis lazuli* to align with the highest spiritual energies.

Essential Oils

Clove to drive away hostile and negative forces and to uplift your energy. *Eucalyptus* to remove emotional cords, reduce reactivity, release anger, and deflect untrustworthy people. *Geranium* to invoke guardians of protection and keep negative energy at bay. *Mandarin* to elicit feelings of safety, to increase mental clarity, and to focus on the positive to counteract the negative. *Palo santo*, derived from sacred wood, to remove unhealthy cords of attachment and clear out negative emotions and paranoia. *Pine* to cleanse and freshen your personal space, clear and relax the mind and the emotions, and remove people who aren't for your highest good. *Rosemary* to release jealousy, clear out negativity, and align your emotional body to attract loyal, authentic, supportive friends and family. *Sage* to clear out negativity, increase feelings of protection, and improve awareness. *Sweet marjoram* to release paranoia, emotional hysteria, and conscious and subconscious fears and to shore up inner strength and courage.

Supportive Archangels

Archangel Michael for protection and removal of fears, phobias, and obsessions. *Archangel Sabrael* to repel jealousy and negative forces.

Suggested Petition

Oh, Angel of Protection! Please gather a legion of angels to create and amplify a protective shield around me. Keep me safe! Please ward off jealousy and psychic attacks and amplify blessings and well-being. Help me to be mindful of the energetic connections between others and myself. Motivate me to sever unhealthy cords of attachment. Help people who have ill wishes toward me or others turn their focus to self-love and compassion. Help me forgive anyone who acts negatively toward me—either known or unknown—and pray with me to nullify unhealthy and unwelcome energies. Help me overcome feelings of vulnerability and empower me to engage my inner strength. Thank you!

Affirmations

I am protected from negative influences. I am mindful of the energetic connections between others and myself. I automatically remove unhealthy cords of attachment that affect me mentally, emotionally, physically, and spiritually. Challenging situations are transformed and the good is revealed. I am always divinely protected. Only goodness and love are allowed in my space.

ANGEL OF RECEIVING

*A*m I giving too much of myself? Do I feel like I am giving and giving but not receiving? Am I open to receive friendship, blessings, gifts, help, love, and all that is good?

Call on the Angel of Receiving when you realize that you're giving a lot but you aren't receiving anything in return. It's one thing to be selfless and give without expectation of personal gain or a return, but it's another to block that return from coming your way. Selflessness is altruistic, but there comes a time when doing so empties out your energy and your resources, leaving you to feel disappointment or lack of acknowledgment. The Angel of Receiving is available to help you connect with self-love and the value of reciprocity. Healthy exchange without expectation is beneficial for all concerned. Showing appreciation, support, and gratitude allows for healthy reciprocity. Ask this angel to help you open your energy up to a balanced flow of receiving blessings and support as well as giving these things to others. It is time to open your heart to receive as much as you give!

Chakras

Heart chakra to keep an awareness on having an open heart to allow love. *Solar plexus chakra* to increase feelings of worthiness to receive blessings in your life.

Colors

Green to embrace and accept blessings of loving kindness and abundance. *Pink* to feel nurturing and comforting energy from your circle of friends, family, and community.

Gemstones

Amethyst to receive intuitive insights and guidance. *Botswana agate* to gain wisdom from spiritual teachings. *Green tourmaline* to allow the Universe's infinite gifts of abundance to flow through you for the benefit of all. *Moldavite* to be open to receiving blessings that seemingly come out of nowhere. *Pink tourmaline* for the ability to receive unconditional love and emotional comfort. *Ruby in zoisite* to receive healing vibrations and perceive life through the eyes of love. *Scolecite* to receive information from higher realms of consciousness and through the dreamtime. *Watermelon tourmaline* for assistance in receiving love, compassion, kindness, and thoughtful actions from others.

Essential Oils

Allspice to encourage abundance, prosperity, and plenitude in all areas of your life. *Basil* for support in bringing your ideas and projects into reality with success and financial abundance. *Grapefruit*, especially the pink variety, to open your heart to receive blessings, joy, and happiness. *Hyacinth* for self-acceptance and support from others with regard to your emotions. *Jasmine* to help open your heart, renew self-confidence, and embrace the expression of gratitude. *Orange* to receive love, nurturing, and appreciation in your life from others.

Supportive Archangels

Archangel Auriel aligns your energy to be receptive due to the connection with the Divine Feminine. *Archangel Gabriel* to receive communication, support, and inspiration from the Divine. *Archangel Jophiel* for beauty and support all around you.

Suggested Petition

Oh, Angel of Receiving! Please help me to be open to receiving blessings and appreciation from others. Lately I've felt a bit disillusioned by the lack of gratitude and reciprocity, even though I give without expectations of receiving from that same source. Show me how to balance my energy so it is easy for me to receive. I want to have healthy boundaries so others don't take advantage of my good nature. Reveal to me the ways in which reciprocity and gratitude are working in my life, especially when the blessings are coming from people or situations that are seemingly unrelated to where I've been generous and giving. Thank you!

Affirmations

I am willing to receive love. The door to my heart is open. Blessings flow into my life. I accept gifts, love, and attention with ease and grace. I am grateful for all that is bestowed upon me. My life flows easily with grace. The energy of healing, love, and well-being flows through me.

ANGEL OF RECOVERY

*W*hat am I recovering from? Am I allowing myself the time it takes to rebalance and reestablish my equilibrium? How can I best heal from this period of intensity?

Call on the Angel of Recovery when you are going through a physical healing, an emotional rebalancing, a financial reestablishment, or a time of restoration after extreme heartache and sorrow. Whether you are recovering from an addiction to a substance or recovering from something else that has been removed from your life, this angel can lend support during the time it takes to restore your body, mind, and soul. Full recovery includes a detox of your mind and removal of repetitive negative thought patterns. Be willing to ask for the support you need to help you break free from anything that is holding you back from living a happy life. Ask the Angel of Recovery to help you find ways to integrate spirituality into your life so that you can feel fulfilled and supported by the Divine.

Chakras

Crown chakra to connect your highest version of yourself with conscious awareness. *Solar plexus chakra* to integrate the situations that are in process and allow for your confidence and courage to rise up to life's circumstances. *Third eye chakra* to go within yourself for contemplative thought and to quiet your mind for peace and tranquility. *Throat chakra* to improve your ability to communicate what you are feeling and to express yourself with ease.

Colors

Black to mourn life changes. *Brown* to remember to spend time in nature as part of the recovery process. *Green* to remain loving and kind to yourself. *Pink* to allow for tears and comfort to be a normal part of the process. *Purple* to transform and transmute challenging experiences and feelings. *Yellow* to process, digest, and release the old way of being with mercy and kindness toward yourself.

Gemstones

Amethyst to support you as you heal from any kind of addiction or bad habit. *Citrine* to easily process and release toxins as well as toxic thoughts to regain your center of personal power. *Phantom quartz* to support recovery from the habitual use of drugs, alcohol, or any overused substance. *Phosphosiderite* to feel comfort and restore balance after a period of grief following a loss or disappointment. *Rhodonite* for restoration and healing through nourishment, levity, and balance.

Essential Oils

Juniper berry to detoxify your body, cleanse your aura, and support your spiritual connection. *Lemon* to restore vitality, release physical exhaustion, and refresh the body on all levels following a prolonged illness. *Lemongrass* to restore balance, process surrounding circumstances, and increase joyfulness and enthusiasm after a stressful period. *Pine* for cleansing, purifying, and keeping out negative psychic energy and unwanted influences.

Supportive Archangels

Archangel Jophiel to heal your thoughts and to refocus your attention on health and well-being. *Archangel Michael* to battle and remove all inner or outer demons. *Archangel Raphael* to cleanse and regenerate, thereby effectuating healing on all levels—mentally, emotionally, physically, and spiritually. *Archangel Uriel* to understand repetitive patterns and move on from them.

Suggested Petition

Oh, Angel of Recovery! Please help me to take a look at where I've been and realize that there is so much more I can do, learn, and experience by releasing patterns of abuse or overuse that are not for my highest good. Please bring me a circle of supportive colleagues and friends who are compassionate and empathetic as I heal through the processes of recovery. Please show me how to improve my ability to deal with difficult feelings and emotions. Give me the tools to cope and carry on. Thank you!

Affirmations

I fully appreciate my transformation. My emotions are balanced, and I enjoy this state of being. Events from my past positively affect my present and future. I embrace change. I recognize that change can usher in improved life situations. My body is in a constant state of restoration and healing. My mental and emotional bodies are nourished and balanced. I find balance in my life through play, work, rest, exercise, and laughter. I easily nurture myself. I attract nurturing people into my life.

ANGEL OF RELATIONSHIPS

*A*m I allowing love into my life? Do I seek out new friends and companions or do I wait until they reach out to me? Do I need to heal wounds from previous relationships to feel safe enough to venture into new friendships and romance?

Call on the Angel of Relationships when you feel like you don't have the types of close-knit friendships you desire. With this angel's assistance, you can delve into unresolved emotions and proceed toward emotional healing. Make a decision to discontinue unwanted repetitive patterns in your relationships so that your future interactions are healthy and uplifting. Evaporate old, teary emotions and release the charge or cords of attachment from past relationship experiences so that those experiences do not bias or color any new relationships that come your way. Allow this angel to help you heal and release past emotional wounds and to teach you to open yourself up to enriching love and friendship. This angel can also help you enter into new romantic relationships without letting past experiences get in the way of finding true love, support, and fulfillment.

Chakras

Heart chakra to open your energy to receive support, love, friendship, and romance. *Navel chakra* to find creative ways to connect with others. *Solar plexus chakra* for self-confidence and the ability to set boundaries.

Colors

Green to open your heart to love, kindness, and connection with yourself and others. *Pink* to activate the receptive energy of support and comfort in relationships. *Red* to help you take action and move forward. *Yellow* to increase self-esteem and personal power.

Gemstones

Danburite to overcome negative thoughts about yourself and to increase success in beneficial relationships. *Elestial quartz* to heal yourself of emotional wounds and improve self-esteem. *Kunzite* to maintain a loving vibration at all times. *Pink calcite* to allow loving kindness into your life. *Rose quartz* to amplify love for self and others. *Septarian* to embrace your self-worth and your magnificence. *Seraphinite* to cut cords still clinging to you from past relationships.

Essential Oils

Geranium to find balance through play and laughter with your beloved and/or dear friends. *Grapefruit* to develop a stronger sense of self, rid your emotional body of doubt and fear, and cultivate trust as you develop loving relationships. *Hyacinth* to transform sad thoughts of past relationships into happy, nostalgic memories. *Orange* to open your heart to receive love, nurturing, and comfort in your life from yourself and others. *Pine* for when you are feeling that you will have an emotional breakdown. It helps you release feelings of resentment, self-pity, and bitterness. *Rosemary* to align with everlasting love and loyalty. *Rosewood* to encourage loyal relationships and increase feelings of worthiness.

Supportive Archangels

Archangel Chamuel to amplify blessings and well-being in relationships. *Archangel Haniel* to improve communication skills. *Archangel Seraphiel* to release personal and family karma.

Suggested Petition

Oh, Angel of Relationships! Please help me cultivate a wonderful group of friends and colleagues in my life with courage and confidence. Help me shift my energy to allow me to receive love and take steps to do my part in nurturing loyal, caring friendships. Please help me open my heart and have the strength to overcome shyness or a lack of self-esteem so that I can take action to develop strong, healthy connections with great friends and family, including my romantic relationship. Thank you!

Affirmations

I am love. All that surrounds me and all that is attracted to me is love. I attract loyal, authentic friends and romantic relationships. I am blessed with supportive friends. I am grateful for companionship in my life. My friendships and business relationships are important to me. I take steps to cultivate close-knit bonds with the people in my life.

ANGEL OF RELAXATION

*A*m I going in too many directions at once and feeling energetically depleted? Am I able to let go of all that needs to be done? How do I release all my thoughts and worries for a while?

Call on the Angel of Relaxation when you just can't seem to stop doing and thinking and you feel emotionally, mental, physically, or spiritually overwhelmed. Ask for help to stop and just "be." Imagine yourself at peace with nothing to do. Use the power of creative visualization to see yourself reclining on a lounge chair, receiving a massage, or however you feel you can best achieve a feeling of total relaxation. Brainstorm ways you can stop the constant motion of your body and your mind and then let yourself experience one of them. Decide to pause for little intervals of mindful meditation—even five minutes at a time—to practice "not doing." Taking the time to pause your activities and relax can help you to replenish your energy and perhaps see the challenges before you from a clearer, more centered perspective. Simply ask the Angel of Relaxation to help you make this possible.

Chakras

Crown chakra to make a connection with a higher power, which elicits a sense of calm. *Heart chakra* to stay focused on love and comfort. *Third eye chakra* to remember to take time to quiet your mind and rest.

Colors

Light blue to invite restful and peaceful feelings. *Light pink* for comfort and compassion for yourself and others.

Gemstones

Apophyllite for mental clarity and deeper understanding. *Axinite* to help you relax when you feel challenged by scattered forces—from within and also from outside of yourself. *Chrysocolla* to give yourself the time for shamanic journeywork or to engage in deep meditative practices. *Chrysoprase* to nurture yourself through rest by taking good care of your body, mind, and spirit. *Larimar* to invoke the calming energy of the gentle ebb and flow of waves on the seashore.

Essential Oils

Clary sage to release stress and to bring about a sense of serenity. *Eucalyptus* to encourage the use of the breath and to clear energetic space. *Lavender* to soothe worrisome emotions and experience tranquility and inner peace. *Neroli* to rebalance emotions and support Divine Feminine energy. *Orange* to invite comfort and ease into your life. *Sweet marjoram* to release subconscious fears and relax the mental body enough so that you can let go of negative thoughts associated with fears, phobias, and obsessions.

Supportive Archangels

Archangel Chamuel to bring peace to your relationships so that you can relax. *Archangel Gabriel* to be in a receptive space of being and not doing. *Archangel Jophiel* to willingly take the time to observe beauty and blessings in your surroundings. *Archangel Michael* to feel divinely protected and safe. *Archangel Raphael* to feel healthy, whole, and complete.

Suggested Petition

Oh, Angel of Relaxation! Please help me slow down. Bring my awareness to a place of peace and serenity. I want to experience tranquility. Please help me enrich my spiritual life with inner peace. I need assistance to relax long enough to deepen my understanding of spiritual lessons. I am asking for help to have the courage to stop thinking and meditate. Guide me to renew my body, mind, and spirit by setting aside the necessary time. Help me find the value in doing nothing. Thank you!

Affirmations

I take the time to rest, regroup, and rejuvenate. I allow myself to rest and do nothing. I regularly experience deep healing and restorative meditations. Guided imagery escorts me along a path of peace, goodness, and well-being. It is easy for me to quiet my mind. I give myself permission to stop doing and just be.

ANGEL OF RETIREMENT

*A*m I financially and emotionally ready to retire and find a new identity outside of my work? Do I have enough hobbies to enjoy leaving the workforce? Are there things on my bucket list that I want to do once I retire?

Call on the Angel of Retirement when you start to think about leaving the workforce and transitioning into the next phase of your life. With the help of the Angel of Retirement, you can uncover a new identity for yourself that exists separately from your work life. Ask for the help you need to clearly analyze your financial situation so that you have plenty of money and resources to relax into an enjoyable future, free of the burden of financial uncertainty. Take the time to calculate potential income to be sure you can afford to retire. Imagine that this angel is by your side as you seek an understanding about pensions, healthcare costs, long-term care policies, and applying for government support benefits so that you can step into retirement feeling prepared and well-informed. This angel is your ally as you process the emotions associated with walking away from your career.

Chakras

Crown chakra to be consciously awake and involved in living life to the fullest. *Heart chakra* to amplify loving kindness in all that you do. *Root chakra* to have vitality, flexibility, and endurance.

Colors

Green for heart-centered focus and happiness. *Red* for vitality and a strong financial foundation. *Silver* to align with higher understanding and wisdom.

Gemstones

Emerald for good health, enhanced memory and mental clarity, healthy emotional balance, and extreme wealth. *Ruby* to encourage vitality and vibrant living and to increase abundance, safety, and the motivation to be a productive member of the community. *Sapphire* for mental clarity and to recognize the wisdom garnered from years of work experience.

Essential Oils

Anise seed for healthy digestion and integration of life as it continues anew. *Basil* for good memory, mental clarity, and focus. *Celery seed* to ward off arthritis and gout. *Cinnamon* to maintain a healthy appetite. *Lavender* for restful sleep and calm demeanor. *Lemongrass* for supple muscles and general well-being. *Rosemary* to feel clear mentally and energized physically.

Supportive Archangels

Archangel Ariel for general health and vitality. *Archangel Gabriel* for guidance and inner knowing. *Archangel Haniel* for alignment with your soul's purpose so that you can continue to fulfill it for the remainder of this life. *Archangel Melchizedek* to light the path of your spiritual journey and to activate the mystic within. *Archangel Metatron* to realize and understand the evolution of your soul from a much higher perspective. *Archangel Raziel* for sage wisdom and a deeper understanding of the Great Mystery.

Suggested Petition

Oh, Angel of Retirement! Please help me through this next chapter of my life so that I can experience a happy and enjoyable retirement. I need help discovering who I am separate from my career. Inspire me to continue to be a vital part of my community. Show me how to manage my money so that I have abundant finances for the rest of my days. Help me learn about senior citizen discounts so I can save money on the ordinary things. Provide me with the motivation to maintain and improve my health, strength, and vitality. Thank you!

Affirmations

I consciously embrace the wisdom I have garnered throughout my life. I continue to be a fruitful member of my community. I am aligned with my soul's purpose. I am connected with powerful ancient wisdom. I enjoy retirement. I now have plenty of time to pursue the hobbies that bring me joy. I am looking forward to spending more time with the people I love.

ANGEL OF ROMANCE

*H*ow do I want to experience romance? Am I open to feeling the excitement and mystery of love? Have I taken the time to look at what didn't work in the past and focus on what I want in a future intimate relationship with a romantic partner?

Call on the Angel of Romance when you are yearning for a deeper romantic relationship or when you are ready to initiate a new partnership. This angel will help you achieve clarity and maintain focus on how you want to feel in this romantic emotional connection. Decide how you want to be wooed. Though romance is a mystical experience, carefully consider all the elements of the kind of romance you want for yourself. Take steps to start treating yourself the way you want to be treated by a romantic partner. Observe how you speak to yourself or think of yourself so that you can make positive adjustments so that your romantic partner reflects the positive back to you. Honor and respect yourself as you would have others honor and respect you. Be open to self-reflection so you can give the kind of healthy love and support you want to receive from your partner.

Chakras

Crown chakra to always remember to keep a place in your union for the Divine. *Heart chakra* to maintain focus on love. *Root chakra* for grounded, healthy sex. *Solar plexus chakra* to maintain confidence throughout the relationship and ease in setting boundaries in a healthy way.

Colors

Green to maintain heart-centered focus filled with loving kindness. *Red* for passion and sensuous lovemaking. *Pastel blue* to encourage honest communication, to be a good listener, and to find the best manner to express yourself to your partner. *Pink* to consciously be a loving partner and to remember to show love to your partner. *Yellow* to aid in maintaining your own sense of self and to be who you truly are throughout your times together.

Gemstones

Blue lace agate to improve your ability to communicate and speak your truth so that you are heard and understood, including by yourself. *Citrine* to remember that it is safe for you to be powerful and self-confident in your relationship. *Danburite* to connect with your highest vibration and to allow you to attract high-vibration romance. *Emerald* to heal negative emotions and to maintain an open heart to give and receive. *Hiddenite* to boost your magnetic vibration to attract romance and love. *Kunzite* to attract a supportive and loving romance of high moral standards and to encourage kindness, compassion, and tolerance. *Pink calcite* to alleviate feelings of hurt, fear, anger, and frustration. *Rose quartz* to attract romance, good friends, and love. *Sapphire* to invite wisdom and extraordinary loyalty into your relationship.

Essential Oils

Bergamot for an optimistic outlook and for improving levels of joy and self-confidence. *Clary sage* to cultivate tools to love and be loved without neediness and balanced detachment. *Geranium* to cancel out angry, vindictive, or negative thoughts, which helps during heated disagreements. *Neroli* for improving fertility due to its relaxing effects and ability to enhance sexual desire. *Pink grapefruit* for joy, clarity, and heart-centered focus. *Rosemary* to enhance loyalty and fidelity. *Ylang-ylang* to help calm erratic emotions, to heighten sexual desire, and for fertility.

Supportive Archangels

Archangel Auriel to release worries, negative thoughts, and fears that could sabotage your romantic partnership. *Archangel Chamuel* to heal issues from past relationships and free you of old emotional challenges. *Archangel Jophiel* for inner wisdom and beauty. *Archangel Sabrael* to establish a sense of trust and loyalty in your relationship while eliminating feelings of jealousy. *Guardian Angel* to guide you and light your path in alignment with your highest, best good and to help you align with the Guardian Angel of your romantic partner.

Suggested Petition

Oh, Angel of Romance! Please help me be the best romantic partner I can be. Draw to me a romance that is affectionate, supportive, sensual, and sexual. Help me cultivate a mystical, spiritual relationship filled with love, kindness, compassion, and laughter. Show me how I can be grateful for the love that already exists in my life and how to love myself the way I want my romantic partner to love me. Help me align my spiritual heart and mind with my crown and heart chakras to attract or cultivate a deeply fulfilling romantic partnership. Thank you!

Affirmations

I am love, and all that surrounds me and all that is attracted to me is love. I attract love, joy, and happiness into my life. My magnetic vibration attracts romance and love. I am nurturing. I accept nurturing from others. I am compassionate and kind. I give love to others and readily accept their love in return.

ANGEL OF SETTING BOUNDARIES

*H*ow can I keep my sacred space free of argumentative and disrespectful people? Why am I attracting these challenges? Why am I reactive when faced with angry people?

The Angel of Setting Boundaries helps you discern when you need to establish a boundary. This is the angel to call on when you require clarity and the ability to rise above challenging situations instead of buying in to the drama or enabling inappropriate behavior. Learn to set boundaries with people who want to take advantage of you and sweet talk you rather than get angry with you. It is important that your life be free of disrespect and argumentative vibes. Be mindful and let go of reacting to other people's anger. This allows you to be aware that you have an opportunity to be loving, kind, and peaceful in the face of the discomfort. Remember that your true nature is love, and you choose how you react to other people. Instead of reacting to unpleasant people, take a moment to breathe and say a little prayer for them and for yourself.

Chakras

Heart chakra to maintain ease and grace. *Navel chakra* to have the courage to take action to establish boundaries. *Solar plexus chakra* for confidence and inner strength. *Throat chakra* to be able to speak up for yourself.

Colors

Blue calms the angry energy. *Yellow* to have confidence in your personal power.

Gemstones

Amber to experience a strong sense of self and express it with wisdom. *Angelite* to call in the support of your spiritual entourage to comfort you during a potentially difficult experience. *Azurite-malachite* to instill peace and calm within. *Celestite* for ease in communicating your truth to others. *Chrysocolla* to lessen the potential for using anger as a tool to set a boundary. *Citrine* to activate your self-confidence and self-esteem. *Honey calcite* for calm emotions, a peaceful demeanor, and the focus to realize you are the only one who is responsible for what happens to you and around you. *Lapis lazuli* to maintain a calm and wise vibration. *Sapphire* to be loyal to yourself by affirming your needs and desires.

Essential Oils

Amber to encourage feelings of protection and empowerment. *Chamomile* to allay intense emotions and outbursts. *Elemi* to instill a detached perspective, increase unwaveringness, and filter fearful feelings. *Lavender* for comfort and to soothe and calm hysteria and chaotic emotions.

Supportive Archangels

Archangel Metatron for discernment and the strength to set boundaries. *Archangel Seraphiel* to feel empowered to set boundaries with family members and release familial karma.

Suggested Petition

Oh, Angel of Setting Boundaries! Please help me speak my truth when I need to set a boundary in my life. It is important to my well-being that my life is free of disrespect and argumentative vibes. Show me how to peacefully interact with others when they are argumentative and/or disrespectful of me, my space, my home, or my place of business. Please help me observe aggressive behavior within myself to transform mannerisms and tone of voice so that interactions are harmonious and mutually respectful. Help me to be less reactive and have an awakened heart. Thank you!

Affirmations

I have the courage to set boundaries with love and grace. I have a strong sense of self. I am protected from others who might violate my boundaries, either knowingly or unknowingly. I am empowered by past experiences. I am connected to powerful ancient wisdom that I can use for beneficial purposes. I know how to make positive changes. It is safe to be powerful in loving ways.

ANGEL OF SOUND SLEEP

*W*hat prevents me from having sound sleep? Why do I wake up in the middle of the night? Why do I have difficulty falling asleep and/or going back to sleep?

The Angel of Sound Sleep helps you make adjustments to your life so that you are free of troublesome thoughts and feelings. This angel is associated with the Angel of Awakening, the Angel of the Dreamtime, and the Angel of Meditation and Contemplation, since you need to quiet your mind to achieve deep enough sleep, which is connected with dreams and realizations. Being at peace with yourself allows you to relax your body, mind, and spirit. This angel is the one to call on to orchestrate your day and your night so that you instill the habits necessary for you to experience the benefits of deep, restful sleep. Ask the Angel of Sound Sleep to help you implement any changes you need to make regarding food, drink, and your environment so you can get to sleep, stay asleep, and sleep better.

Chakras

Crown chakra to align with your higher consciousness to clear away subconscious thoughts. With mental clarity and inner peace, sleep is better. *Third eye chakra* to access the quiet mind and connection to dreaming.

Colors

Pastel blue for tranquility and peace. *Pastel pink* for nurturing, comforting energy. *Purple* to release repetitive thoughts.

Gemstones

Amethyst to transmute troublesome thoughts and emotions, thereby encouraging peaceful sleep. *Apophyllite* for dreaming and a conscious sleeping experience. *Hematite* to feel safe and grounded as you drift off to sleep. *Purple-dyed agate* to shift into a peaceful state when you close your eyes. *Rose quartz* to feel covered in a blanket of love and comfort. *Scolecite* to improve your ability to transition from one state of consciousness to another—from sleep to wakefulness and vice versa.

Essential Oils

Chamomile to encourage wisdom teachings to come through your dreams. *Lavender* to soothe and relieve stress and bring about a sense of peace, calm, and restfulness. *Mandarin* for restful sleep. *Melissa*, also known as *lemon balm*, to encourage you to take the time to smell the sweetness of life around you. *Sweet marjoram* for feelings of safety, to calm emotions, and to promote healthy breathing and restorative sleep.

Supportive Archangels

Archangel Jophiel for a restful sleep that rejuvenates and regenerates you. *Archangel Raphael* to encourage self-healing as you sleep. *Guardian Angel* to guard you throughout the night.

Suggested Petition

Oh, Angel of Sound Sleep! As I drift off to sleep, please help me let go of the day's stress, quiet angry and hurt feelings, and release the incessant chatter in my mind. Watch over me while I sleep. Guide my dreams to help me process my thoughts and emotions. Let your caring presence be the comfort I need in order to rest fully so that my body, mind, and spirit are renewed when I wake up. Thank you!

Affirmations

I am mindful of being in peaceful places that support my loving vibration. I take good care of myself. I sleep well every night. Peace and serenity are mine. I relax and breathe deeply, knowing all is well. I am grateful for sound sleep and pleasant dreams.

ANGEL OF TRANSFORMATION

*W*hat do I need to transform? What isn't working for me—mentally, physically, spiritually, and emotionally? How can I transmute challenging situations?

Call on the Angel of Transformation when it is time to transform your situation. Usually the transformation is connected to the relationship you have with yourself, as well as the relationships you have with others. This angel helps you examine your actions, thoughts, feelings, and reactions so you are better able to align yourself with an objective view of the truth. A deeper understanding of the relationship you have with yourself, how you think about yourself, and how you think about others is essential for the spiritual growth you need to transform your reality into one of joy and happiness. While the transformation process can be a bit uncomfortable at times, with heightened awareness of your thoughts, attitudes, and feelings the way can be much easier. The path to the future will be filled with good intentions and actualized dreams.

Chakras

Crown chakra for clarity of thinking. *Third eye chakra* to use your spiritual eyes to have a greater perspective and advanced hindsight. *Throat chakra* to hear and know messages from the Divine via the angels.

Colors

Black for protection during the process of transformation. *Purple* to envision a swirly cloak of transformational light around you.

Gemstones

Amethyst to transform challenging situations. *Gabbro indigo* to shape-shift any situation with positive energy. *Purple-dyed agate* to transform negative thoughts and belief systems into their positive counterparts. *Silver-sheen obsidian* to deflect negativity and to improve the ability to recognize how the situation mirrors something deep within your soul that needs to be healed.

Essential Oils

Benzoin to feel safe and protected as you spiral toward higher consciousness as part of your evolution. *Bergamot* to improve your confidence to traverse the transformational process. *Grapefruit* to commune with higher realms of consciousness and wisdom to better understand the bigger picture. *Palo santo* to align with the sacredness of all life. *Pine* for a clear path sweetened with success and blessings for everyone involved. *Rosemary* to deepen your understanding of the power generated by rites of passage as well as the cycles of life. *Sweet marjoram* to calmly realign yourself during periods of adjustment and transformation.

Supportive Archangels

Archangel Metatron to raise your consciousness for awareness of the bigger picture. *Archangel Michael* for Divine protection and the ability to rise above situations. *Archangel Raphael* to support the process of healing through changes. *Archangel Zadkiel* for transformation and transmutation for spiritual alchemy.

Suggested Petition

Oh, Angel of Transformation! I am in the midst of life-changing experiences, and I am afraid of the unknown. Please increase my faith and help me to be steadfast and resolute during this time of transformation. Help me transmute any situations that are no longer for my highest good into positive lessons. Enlighten me with the foresight and wisdom of how these transformations will be beneficial for my life over the long run. I want to focus on all that is good, and I need help to do that during this time of great change. Thank you!

Affirmations

I am safe. It's easy for me to transmute challenging situations into beneficial circumstances. I have the tools to transform negative thought patterns into positive ones. I overcome challenges with ease and grace. I fully appreciate my transformation. Events from my past positively affect my present and future. I embrace change. I recognize that change can usher in improved life situations.

ANGEL OF TRANSITION

*I*s there a part of my life that is passing away? Who or what is transitioning out of my world? Do I need to make some changes to move things in ways that are for my highest good?

The Angel of Transition lights your path as parts of your life here on Earth reach completion or die away. This angel is the one to help spirits and disincarnate entities, including our loved ones (people and animals alike), find their way to the Other Side. It guides, comforts, and supports them on their sacred journey to their next realm of consciousness. This angel will be there for you when it is time to depart from this world. This celestial guide is filled with loving kindness and knows when it is time to open the portal into the next dimension. The Angel of Transition also calls on the legions of Angels of Comfort to assist those remaining here on Earth. This angel also helps you transition from one life path to another as the course of your life changes, helping you release what no longer serves you and appreciate those parts of your past that have guided you forward thus far.

Chakras

Crown chakra for awakened consciousness to remember why you are here and where you are going. *Navel chakra* to focus on your core strength and creative views on life. *Solar plexus chakra* to connect with your inner power. *Third eye chakra* for clarity on your soul's journey through many lives.

Colors

Gold to activate action and awareness from one path to the next. *Iridescent purple* to encourage good energy and positive transformation. *White* to light the way to understanding and wisdom.

Gemstones

Ammonite to spiral into the center of your consciousness to recognize where you are in the ever-turning wheel of life. *Elestial quartz* to encourage the angels to orchestrate the transition process for the highest good of all. *Isis quartz* to understand the impermanent nature of life. *Time link quartz* to confidently step forth with an understanding that events link together to create the greater plan.

Essential Oils

Frankincense to receive insights and realizations through universal consciousness for greater cosmic understanding. *Jasmine* for healing and to embrace the sweetness of all life while going through the process of transforming your reality. *Rosemary* for protection during transformational rites of passage. *Sandalwood* for calm, inner wisdom, and loving kindness.

Supportive Archangels

Archangel Gabriel to trumpet the way forward with clarity. *Archangel Metatron* for ease in your soul's evolution. *Archangel Raziel* to align with revelation and the Great Mystery. *Archangel Uriel* to bring you an understanding of the universal flow.

Suggested Petition

Oh, Angel of Transition! Please shine light on my path as I stand at the gateway of this transition. Help me find my way and recognize where I am, where I am going, and how to get there. Allow me to be of assistance to others as they go through transitions in their life, including as they prepare to depart from this earthly existence. Comfort me and help me to realize we are never alone and that help is always available. Thank you!

Affirmations

I accept the impermanent nature of life and embrace transitions. I assist people who are challenged by the changes they face. I acknowledge transition as a loss of something and embrace the grieving process. I easily adapt to my changing environment and effortlessly transition from one state of being to the next. Change is good.

ANGEL OF
UNCONDITIONAL LOVE

*A*m I willing to accept affection, love, and attention without any limitations? Is there someone in my life I want to accept me just as I am? Do I need to love myself more and honor myself for who I am without feeling a need to change myself?

Invite the Angel of Unconditional Love to help and guide you when you are seeking acceptance of yourself and others. Ask this angel to help others demonstrate the love they have for you and to show you the ways you can open yourself to become a receptacle for all that is love. This angel can assist you in becoming aware of the many people who love you exactly as you are without judgment. Remember, good fortune and blessings are often the result of years of good thoughts, good deeds, hard work, and an open heart. Practice gratitude. The Angel of Unconditional Love is also an ally for you when you need to repent or forgive—or potentially both. Let this angel help you hone your ability to release feelings of resentment, anger, or negativity toward yourself or another person. This angel can help guide you toward demonstrating your love to others in a way that is enriching, both to them and to yourself.

Chakras

Crown chakra to realize the unconditional love of the Divine. *Heart chakra* to align with mercy, compassion, kindness, forgiveness, and repentance. *Third eye chakra* to recognize unconditional love in its many forms.

Colors

Green to experience nurturing energy and the support of loving friends and family. *Pink* to receive comforting love and emotional support.

Gemstones

Cobaltoan calcite to align with the ultimate recognition of unconditional love, mercy, and understanding. *Dalmatian jasper* to appreciate and learn from the unconditional love and loyalty of our adoring animal companions. *Epidote* to remind yourself that there is plenty of everything for everyone, especially unconditional love. *Magenta-dyed agate* to increase emotional maturity and accept both the negative and positive aspects of yourself and others. *Watermelon tourmaline* to embrace all aspects of your human nature.

Essential Oils

Clary sage to ground feelings and emotions and to bring about a sense of serenity. *Lavender* to clear and calm the mind and comfort your heart.

Supportive Archangels

Archangel Chamuel to open your heart center and activate loving vibrations. *Archangel Muriel* to bring emotional balance to experience unconditional love. *Archangel Raphael* to heal and open your heart to feel love.

Suggested Petition

Oh, Angel of Unconditional Love! Please let me be a conduit for love, compassion, and kindness. Open my heart center at the core of my consciousness to allow heaven and earth to meet at my center. Help me see myself and others through the vibration of love, and allow love to permeate all facets of my life. Guide me so that I take the time to nurture myself and regard myself with honor and respect. Thank you!

Affirmations

I am love. I align my consciousness with gentleness, compassion, and goodwill toward all. I am compassionate and kind. I am aligned with the healing powers of inner peace and kindness. I am able to help others by vibrating love through my presence, words, and actions.

CONCLUSION

*W*ith this book in hand, you have all the tools you need to establish a strong connection with the everyday angels and many of the archangels. It is my hope that you find comfort in knowing that you have an entourage of heavenly helpers available to you every day and night. Imagine the angels helping you with all aspects of your life—big and small life challenges as well as the joys and triumphs of living here on Earth.

Relax and allow life to unfold as you employ the spiritual tools of intention: gemstones, aromatherapy, and the power of your spoken word. Use the questions as fodder for contemplative thought and use the affirmations to cultivate your crystal-clear intentions.

Talk to your angels. They are waiting for instructions. Remember to ask the angels for their help and guidance so they can light your path and bring you inspiration. They need a very clear request, so state your goals and objectives and assign them the task of showing you the way for the highest and best good of all concerned. Focus on love, light, joy, laughter, and happiness.

May your days be filled with blessings and love, and may the angels light your path.

APPENDIX A:
SUPPORTIVE ARCHANGELS
EASY-REFERENCE

*T*his appendix material gives a better understanding of the supportive angels. Here you'll find a list of the various archangels that are included throughout the book, along with a brief bio and their areas of expertise.

Archangel Ariel helps to increase motivation, vitality, and vigor. This archangel is a patron of animals and dedicated to protecting the earth's environment and its many animal inhabitants. Archangel Ariel is available to guide you to trust your intuitive realization and provides the courage to act upon that knowledge.

Archangel Auriel is aligned with the Divine Feminine. Archangel Auriel helps you have a healthy mind and enthusiastic outlook and helps you to release subconscious fears. Look to Archangel Auriel to maintain a focus on compassion and mercy. Archangel Auriel is considered to be associated with, or another aspect of, Archangel Uriel.

Archangel Avartiel to ward off miscarriages and protect both men and women during pregnancy.

Archangel Barachiel is portrayed in iconography with a rose or rose petals, symbolizing God's blessings. Call on this archangel for good fortune and to help open your heart to receive abundance. Archangel Barachiel is the chief of the Guardian Angels and is also described as the leader of 496,000 other angels.

Archangel Camael is the angel of strength and courage. There are some texts that consider Camael and Chamuel to be the same archangel. (See below.) Align with Archangel Camael to release anger and inner demons. Archangel Camael helps you to move forward and improve your energy on all levels.

Archangel Chamuel is the angel of peaceful relationships. Chamuel's name means "one who seeks God" and helps you find spiritual connection in all relationships. Call on this archangel to boost your self-confidence to amplify blessings and well-being in relationships, to heal issues from past relationships, and to free yourself of old emotional challenges and petty arguments. Archangel Chamuel helps to open your heart center and activates unconditional love and compassionate action.

Archangel Gabriel is a Divine oracle. He is well-known for the announcement of the birth of the Messiah 200 years before His birth as well as being the angel who appeared to Mother Mary to let her know that she would give birth to Jesus. Call on Archangel Gabriel to open your spiritual ears to hear messages and for inspired guidance, often through symbols and dreams. Archangel Gabriel watches over unborn children and assists in the birth of creative inspiration as manifest reality as well.

Archangel Haniel is an angel of manifestation. Archangel Haniel can help improve your communication skills with animals and all nature. Call on Archangel Haniel to align with your soul's purpose through connection with your higher self. This archangel can help you remember your truth through observation and order.

Archangel Jehudiel strengthens your self-control and ability to overcome poor choices. Jehudiel is the patron of hard work and the patron for those in leadership roles who have great responsibility.

Archangel Jophiel, known as the "beauty of God "or "Divine beauty," is an angel of the seventh heaven, in charge of fifty-three legions of angels, and a guardian of the Torah. Archangel Jophiel inspires you to cultivate good relations with your partner and an abundance of beauty all around you and to help you relax and see the beauty in life.

Archangel Melchizedek helps you correct unpleasant endings and provides insights and esoteric understanding. Use his energy to keep you grounded and safe. Melchizedek was the son of Noah and lived a very long human life—over 500 years. On the other hand, there are accounts that contradict his lineage and consider him an archangel without father, mother, or any genealogy. He is considered a high priest or a priest forever. His name means "king of righteousness." Archangel Melchizedek can shine light on your path for your journey here on Earth and align you with your inner mystic.

Archangel Metatron, formerly known as Enoch, helps you align with higher states of consciousness because he offers a direct connection between the earthly realm and the heavenly realm. Enoch was the great-grandfather of Noah, and he became known as Metatron after his bodily ascent into heaven. He is a celestial scribe. Archangel Metatron is strongly associated with your ability to transform yourself and your life due to his own fiery transformation from Enoch to Metatron. Call on Archangel Metatron to motivate you to take positive action to understand your soul's purpose, to foresee potential future realities, and activate the connection with higher consciousness and your soul's evolution.

Archangel Michael is dedicated to protecting you and helps to remove fears and phobias that might distract you from your intentions. Call on Archangel Michael to bring feelings of comfort and safety. Archangel Michael is often portrayed with silver armor, a round shield, and a sword to ward off malevolent situations, negative people, and inner and outer demons. Archangel Michael can help you to cut the cords of attachment to negative people, places, and situations that are no longer for your highest good. Ask Archangel Michael to help you see life from a higher and greater perspective.

Archangel Muriel's vibration is to instill inner peace and tranquility. The name Muriel is derived from the Greek word *myrrh*. As a biblical oil, myrrh assists you in aligning with the wisdom of Mother Mary, Mary Magdalene, and the Christ consciousness. Archangel Muriel stabilizes and fixes your attention on the vibration of safety and allows you to resolve problems and uncover truths. Use this energy to bring peace and harmony through emotional balance.

Archangel Raphael is the archangel responsible for healing and good health in most traditions. Raphael is mentioned in the Book of Tobit. His name means "it is God who heals." Archangel Raphael provides healing support for any type of discomfort on all levels—mentally, emotionally, physically, and spiritually. This archangel helps to strengthen your determination to overcome health challenges, helps you understand how you created your present situation, and provides healing support through the transformation. Archangel Raphael helps draw helpful people into your life during a period of healing and heals attachments to things that are no longer for your highest good.

Archangel Raziel is the "keeper of secrets" and the "angel of mysteries." Archangel Raziel authored a book containing all secret knowledge that was passed to Adam and Eve, Enoch (later known as Archangel Metatron), and Archangel Raphael, who passed it to Noah for the purpose of having instructions to build the ark. Archangel Raziel can help you embrace and use your spiritual gifts of intuition and prophecy as it relates to being the visionary for your own life. Archangel Raziel can assist you as you awaken to sage wisdom and a deeper understanding of the Great Mystery.

Archangel Sabrael is the guard of the first heaven. This archangel is dedicated to helping release jealousy and preventing negative energy from interfering with your cooperative relationships. Ask this archangel to heal jealousy or envy that stems from you or from outside of you. Archangel Sabrael can help protect your business ideas and property. Archangel Sabrael also wards off incessant mind chatter, which improves meditation and contemplative thought.

Archangel Sachiel increases and manages great success, material gain, extraordinary wealth, and prosperity. Turn to this archangel for good fortune and beneficial outcomes in legal matters. Sachiel means "covering of God" and he is associated with the first heaven. This archangel is in the order of the cherubim. Cherubim are often found interwoven to cover or provide a veil for sacred and valuable objects such as the Tabernacle, the Ark of the Covenant, and the gates of the Garden of Eden. As such, this archangel is your ally to maintain high standards, ethics, and morals aligned with a spiritual foundation.

Archangel Seraphiel incorporates your knowledge and information into your daily decisions in a practical manner. Archangel Seraphiel is referenced in the Book of Enoch and is the protector of Archangel Metatron. He is considered the angel of silence, high rank, and enormous, brilliant light.

Archangel Thuriel is the guardian of animals and helps with interspecies connection, specifically human and animal communication. This is the archangel that encourages outdoor playtime in nature and with animals. Archangel Thuriel is your guide to help you realize how interconnected all life is and how nature, plants, and animals are a major reason to be grateful. This archangel is not found in biblical or theological texts.

Archangel Uriel aids you on your spiritual and intellectual path toward enlightenment and wisdom. Uriel means "God is my light." He is regarded as the keeper of beauty, light, the sun, and the constellations. He is identified as one of the cherubs protecting the Gate of Eden. He is strong and powerful. Archangel Uriel reminds humankind of the importance of planetary citizenship and stewardship. Call on Archangel Uriel for universal flow and to imbue you with a vibe of creative action, prosperity, and wisdom. Archangel Uriel can help transform painful memories and inner conflicts and instills tranquility, freeing you to take action and move forward.

Archangel Zadkiel helps you amplify kindness, mercy, altruism, and thoughtfulness in yourself and those around you. Zadkiel means "righteousness of God" or "grace of God" and is dedicated to freedom and mercy. Call on Archangel Zadkiel for ease in the transformation process. He also aids in sympathy and empathy for others' misfortunes.

Archangel Zaphkiel aids in contemplative thought and stillness. His name means "God's knowledge." Call on Archangel Zaphkiel for greater understanding and mindfulness. This archangel can help you release personal and family karma.

Archangel Zuriel is known for protecting the mother-to-be and providing comfort during childbirth. Zuriel means "my rock is God." He is known as an archangel of wisdom, understanding, and judgment.

Guardian Angel is the angel assigned to you at birth for this lifetime. Your Guardian Angel helps you feel guided and safe as you navigate the changing landscape of your life. Your Guardian Angel lights your path in alignment with your highest and best good.

Appendix B:
Aromatherapy
Resources
and Cautions

*T*here are many opinions and diverse viewpoints on the safe use of essential oils. Through my research I have found that the most controversial subjects are the use of certain essential oils during pregnancy, the use of essential oils internally, and the use of essential oils with children. Professional organizations such as the National Association for Holistic Aromatherapy (NAHA) and the International Federation of Professional Aromatherapists (IFPA) post safety considerations and guidelines for the use of essential oils in all circumstances.

Inhalation as a method of application is a low-risk avenue for most people. Any risk associated with the inhalation method is from prolonged and excessive exposure to the oil vapors.

The age of an individual plays a part in determining the safe usage of essential oils. For example, infants and young children have a higher sensitivity to essential oils than adults. Safe dilutions, according to the NAHA, include "0.5–2.5% depending on the condition." It is best to avoid the use of birch, wintergreen, and peppermint essential oils with youngsters. Also, skin sensitivity is higher in the elderly population, so the dilution for topical application would be increased in such cases.

For the purposes of aromatherapy as presented within this book, my recommendations are as follows:

- Avoid use of essential oils during pregnancy, especially during the first trimester. It has been shown that toxicity during pregnancy arises when certain essential oils are used in large doses. The key is to properly use essential oils as instructed by a skilled therapist. The cautious use of essential oils by a trained therapist can provide comfort and nurturance for a pregnant woman. According to Tisserand and Young, the following essential oils should not be used during pregnancy: wormwood, rue, oak moss, *Lavandula stoechas*, camphor, parsley seed, sage, and hyssop.
- Keep all essential oils out of the reach of children and pets.
- Keep essential oils away from the eyes.
- Do not use the same essential oil for prolonged periods.
- Never place undiluted essential oils on the skin. Always use a carrier oil.
- Never take essential oils internally.

APPENDIX C:
SPRAYS AND MISTS FOR
THE EVERYDAY ANGELS

*A*ll the sprays and mists listed below are The Crystal Garden brand and are hand-blended, hand-bottled, hand-labeled, and capped with mindfulness by me and my loving staff.

The aromatherapy blends in this list are blends I've created over the past twenty years for mental, emotional, physical, and spiritual well-being. Most of these blends have holy waters from many sacred sites and spiritual places around the world. The majority of the holy waters were collected by me before I became an aromatherapist. Now, some of these holy waters are gifts to me from readers, customers, and friends that travel the world. Inevitably, they are included in the blends below and reach many people, blessing them with every spritz. The blends are also delivered to me through meditation, dreams, and clairaudient direction from the heavenly realm.

I am honored to be able to provide these sprays and mists to all who are drawn to use them.

Angel of Abundance and Prosperity

- Astrology Collection—Capricorn Spray for solid action, discipline, and determination.

- Prosperity Mist to help you realize that you are able to make unlimited income doing what you love.

Angel of Action

- Astrology Collection—Aries Spray for the confidence and determination to move toward a desired outcome.
- Root Chakra Spray to be self-motivated to move forward and take action.

Angel of Anger Management

- Euphoria Relaxation Spray to relieve stress and reduce agitation.
- Mother Mary Divine Mother Spray to invite the energy of compassion, peace, and acceptance.

Angel of Animal Companions

- Saint Francis of Assisi Spray to connect with the patron saint of animals and to improve your ability to commune with nature.

Angel of Awakening

- Crown Chakra Spray to activate your crown chakra and to increase your connection with Divine consciousness.

Angel of Balanced Emotions

- Euphoria Essential Oil Blend to reduce the challenges of anxiety, stress, and fear and to improve hormonal balance.
- Calm Spray to feel inner peace and tranquility.

Angel of Blessings

- Ganesha Spray to destroy obstacles in your way and make room for blessings.
- Miracle Water to invoke miracles in your life and to create extraordinary events in the physical world that surpass all known human or natural powers.

Angel of Career

- Prosperity Mist to improve financial success and increase action, self-motivation, abundance, health, and vitality.

Angel of Change

- Ganesha Spray to destroy obstacles and bring forth blessings when changes are necessary.

Angel of Childbirth

- Euphoria Essential Oil Blend to elicit euphoric feelings.
- Calm Spray to promote a deep sense of tranquility.

Angel of Comfort

- Calm Spray to reconnect with trust and faith.
- Lavender Mist to bring forth a feeling of peace.
- Miracle Water to invite the miraculous into your life.

Angel of Communication

- Throat Chakra Spray to pay special attention to how you express yourself.
- Archangel Gabrielle Spray to open your ears, heart, and consciousness to hear and understand others and the Divine.

Angel of Compassion

- Archangel Zadkiel Spray to amplify kindness, mercy, altruism, and thoughtfulness in yourself and those around you.
- Heart Chakra Spray to be compassionate and kind.
- Kuan Yin Goddess of Mercy and Compassion Spray to have mercy and to support those who need a hand.

Angel of Creative Intelligence

- Crown Chakra Spray to access higher wisdom and knowledge.
- Navel Chakra Spray to increase your courage in bringing your ideas into actuality.

Angel of Determination

- Astrology Collection—Aries Spray for confidence, determination, and passion to move toward a desired outcome.
- Root Chakra Spray to stay grounded, but also enthusiastic, when pursuing your determined goal.

Angel of Discernment

- Archangel Metatron Spray to help you with discernment, setting boundaries, mental clarity, and the power to rise above challenging situations.
- Bliss Mist to increase self-confidence and mental clarity.

Angel of Discipline

- Astrology Collection—Capricorn Spray to encourage responsible, productive behavior.
- Archangel Michael Spray to remove fears and phobias that might distract you from your intentions.

Angel of Divine Intervention

- Guardian Angel Spray to help you remember to ask the angels to light your path and show you the way through life.
- Miracle Water to create extraordinary events in the physical world.

Angel of Divine Remembrance

- Crown Chakra Spray to align your higher self to remember your truth.
- Frankincense Mist to align you with higher consciousness for increased awareness and mystical experiences.

Angel of Divine Timing

- Throat Chakra Spray to improve your ability to communicate on the earthly plane as well as with the spiritual realm.

Angel of the Dreamtime

- Archangel Gabrielle Spray to encourage messages and understanding during sleep.
- Be Sleepy Roll On for deep relaxation and a stress-free sleeping experience that encourages dreaming and dream recall.
- Astrology Collection—Pisces Spray to amplify intentions for introspection and intuitive realization through the dreamtime.

Angel of Emotional Maturity

- Euphoria Relaxation Spray to calm and balance your emotions, thereby increasing your emotional maturity.
- Mother Mary Divine Mother Spray to bring balance through the energy of the Divine Feminine, bringing feelings of calm, confidence, and happiness.

Angel of Envy and Jealousy

- Smudge in Spray to clear away negative thoughts and feelings and increase blessings.
- Sage & Cedar Spray to release jealousy and amplify feelings of safety and well-being.

Angel of Fertility

- Euphoria Essential Oil Blend to bring a sense of calm and improve hormone balance.

Angel of Flexibility

- Saint Germain Spray to help you have the willingness to accept change.

Angel of Forgiveness

- Archangel Zadkiel Spray for repentance and forgiveness and to amplify kindness, mercy, altruism, and thoughtfulness in yourself and those around you.
- Heart Chakra Spray to encourage acceptance, compassion, and tolerance.

Angel of Fun and Play

- Guardian Angel Spray to relax into knowing that all is well and that it is safe to enjoy life.

Angel of Good Fortune

- Ganesha Spray to bring forth blessings.
- Prosperity Mist to improve financial success.

Angel of Gratitude

- Ganesha Spray to recognize all the blessings in your life.

Angel of Grief

- Mary Magdalene Spray to align with the eternal nature of each soul.

Angel of a Happy Home

- Saint Joseph Spray to bring good fortune into your home and to the lives of your family.
- Serenity Mist to create feelings of tranquility and peace.
- Smudge in Spray to maintain a space filled with love and clear of negativity.

Angel of Health

- Archangel Raphael Spray to bring connection with the highest level of self-care and healing.

Angel of Helpful People

- Guardian Angel Spray to help you remember that there is always help and hope and that you are never alone.

Angel of Inner Knowing

- Crown Chakra Spray to align with higher consciousness and increase your awareness of the spiritual and mystical experiences of the universe.
- Third Eye Chakra Spray to increase and improve intuition.

Angel of Inner Peace

- Calm Spray to promote balance and tranquility.
- Serenity Mist to bring about feelings of peace and calm.

Angel of Inner Strength

- Bliss Mist to encourage optimism and self-confidence.
- Solar Plexus Chakra Spray to improve determination and courage.

Angel of Intelligence

- Archangel Metatron Spray to connect with higher consciousness and Divine intelligence.
- Crown Chakra Spray to receive and understand higher knowledge.

Angel of Intuition

- Serenity Spray to align you with practices that help you stay focused on your spiritual gifts.
- Third Eye Chakra Spray to improve confidence in your inner knowing.

Angel of Justice

- Archangel Michael Spray to oversee fairness in all situations.
- Ganesha Spray to destroy obstacles and unfairness.

Angel of Loyalty

- Archangel Metatron Spray to align with doing the right thing in any and all circumstances.

Angel of Marriage

- Heart Chakra Spray to amplify your ability to love unconditionally.
- Mary Magdalene Spray to be loved and to be the most beloved.
- Saint Joseph Spray to amplify the best qualities in life partners with a heart-to-heart connection.

Angel of Meditation and Contemplation

- Frankincense Mist to enhance your meditation practice.

- Smudge in Spray to clear away incessant chatter and negative thoughts and to align you with a quiet mind and inner peace.

- Third Eye Chakra Spray to activate and improve your intuition, knowledge, and wisdom.

Angel of Mental Strength

- Crown Chakra Spray to increase your connection with Divine consciousness and the ability to channel and access miracles.

- Eucalyptus Mist to refresh your body, mind, and spirit and clear your mind.

- Third Eye Chakra Spray to activate and improve your intuition, knowledge, and wisdom.

Angel of Nurturing

- Guardian Angel Spray to feel the nurturing presence of your angels.

- Kuan Yin Goddess of Mercy and Compassion Spray to help you feel and act with mercy and compassion and to invite the same in return from others.

- Mother Mary Divine Mother Spray to invite and invoke the energy of compassionate friends, family, and people into your life who are tolerant and accepting of you exactly as you are.

Angel of Opportunity

- Prosperity Mist to open pathways to allow opportunities to unfold.

- Ganesha Spray to destroy obstacles and bring good fortune.

Angel of Order and Organization

- Bliss Mist to establish mental clarity and gain confidence to make decisions.

Angel of Partnership

- Prosperity Mist to focus on passion, motivation, prosperity, health, and vitality.
- Saint Joseph Spray to help with attracting the vibes to support Divine partnership.

Angel of Perspective

- Archangel Michael Spray to align your awareness so you can see the big picture from a higher perspective.
- Third Eye Chakra Spray to activate intuitive knowing, shift your perception, and see varying perspectives.

Angel of Physical Strength

- Bliss Mist for confidence and to align your mind and emotions with the intended goal.
- Eucalyptus Mist to refresh your muscles and clear your mind.
- Root Chakra Spray to recognize and use your core strength.

Angel of Protection

- Archangel Metatron Spray to help you with discernment, setting boundaries, mental clarity, and the power to rise above challenging situations.
- Archangel Michael Spray for peace, protection, justice, goodness, and love.

Angel of Receiving

- Heart Chakra Spray to open yourself to receiving love, nurturing, and appreciation from others.

Angel of Recovery

- Archangel Metatron Spray for the power to rise above challenging situations.
- Saint Germain Spray to alchemize emotions and negative situations.

• Smudge in Spray to clear away negative thoughts and feelings and increase blessings.

Angel of Relationships

• Heart Chakra Spray to activate the heart center and increase feelings of love, mercy, compassion, and kindness.

• Jesus the Christ Spray to be accepting, compassionate, and tolerant.

• Saint Joseph Spray to help with attracting supportive, authentic friendships.

Angel of Relaxation

• Euphoria Relaxation Spray to relieve stress and reduce feelings of agitation.

• Lavender Mist to ease stress and to act as a relaxant and soother.

Angel of Retirement

• Lavender Mist to aid in relaxing into a new way of life.

Angel of Romance

• Heart Chakra Spray to activate the heart center.

• Mary Magdalene Spray to invite the Divine into your romantic relationship.

Angel of Setting Boundaries

• Archangel Metatron Spray to help you with setting boundaries and the power to rise above challenging situations.

Angel of Sound Sleep

• Be Sleepy Roll On to release stress, relax, and feel at peace.

• Guardian Angel Spray to invoke feelings of protection and safety and to help you imagine angels keeping watch over you while you sleep.

Angel of Transformation

- Saint Germain Spray to help you transform and transmute challenging situations.

Angel of Transition

- Miracle Water to create extraordinary events in the physical world that surpass all known human or natural powers.
- Archangel Zadkiel Spray to embrace transformation and to amplify kindness, mercy, and thoughtfulness in yourself and those around you.

Angel of Unconditional Love

- Archangel Zadkiel Spray to allow for the emotional release of potentially poisonous feelings such as resentment, anger, grief, and extreme sadness.
- Kuan Yin Goddess of Mercy and Compassion Spray to help you feel and act with mercy and compassion and to invite the same from others in return.

BIBLIOGRAPHY

Achad, Frater. *Ancient Mystical White Brotherhood.* Lakemont, GA: CSA Press, 1971.

———. *Melchizedek Truth Principles.* Camarillo, CA: DeVorss, 1963.

Castaneda, Carlos. *The Active Side of Infinity.* New York: HarperCollins, 1998.

———. *The Art of Dreaming.* New York: HarperCollins, 1993.

———. *A Separate Reality: Further Conversations with Don Juan.* New York: Penguin Books, 1978.

———. *The Teachings of Don Juan: A Yaqui Way of Knowledge.* Berkeley: University of California Press, 2008.

Caddy, Eileen. *The Spirit of Findhorn.* Forres, Scotland: Findhorn Press, 1994.

Das, Lama Surya. *Awakening the Buddhist Heart: Integrating Love, Meaning, and Connection into Every Part of Your Life.* New York: Broadway Books, 2000.

Davidson, John. *The Secret of the Creative Vacuum: Man and the Energy Dance.* Ashingdon, England: C.W. Daniel, 1989.

Davidson, Gustav. *A Dictionary of Angels: Including the Fallen Angels.* New York: Free Press, 1967.

Day-Schmal, Linda. *Soul-Birthing: How to Choose, Attract, and Influence the Soul of Your Baby Before Conception or Birth.* Sante Fe, NM: SpiritPassage, 1997.

Dionysius the Areopagite. *The Celestial Hierarchy.* Omaha, NE: Patristic Publishing, 2019. Kindle.

Foundation for Inner Peace. *A Course in Miracles.* Novato, CA: Foundation for Inner Peace, 1976.

Gardner-Gordon, Joy. *Color and Crystals: A Journey through the Chakras.* Feasterville-Trevose, PA: Crossing Press, 1988.

Green, Michel. *The Four Archangels: Angelic Inspiration for a Balanced, Joyous Life.* Bloomington, IN: Xlibris, 2010. Kindle.

Hay, Louise. *Heal Your Body.* Carlsbad, CA: Hay House, 1984.

Jordan, Todd. *The Book of Angels.* New York: Sterling, 2006.

Kadmon, Baal. *The 72 Angels of The Name: Calling On the 72 Angels of God.* Self-published, Amazon Digital Services, 2015. Kindle.

Luminare-Rosen, Carista. *Parenting Begins Before Conception: A Guide to Preparing Body, Mind, and Spirit for You and Your Future Child.* Rochester, VT: Healing Arts Press, 2000.

Lembo, Margaret Ann. *The Angels and Gemstone Guardians Cards.* Forres, Scotland: Findhorn Press, 2014.

———. *The Animal Allies and Gemstone Guardians Cards.* Forres, Scotland: Findhorn Press, 2018.

———. *Animal Totems and the Gemstone Kingdom: Spiritual Connections of Crystal Vibrations and Animal Medicine.* Forres, Scotland: Findhorn Press, 2018.

———. *The Archangels and Gemstone Guardians Cards.* Forres, Scotland: Findhorn Press, 2016.

———. *Chakra Awakening: Transform Your Reality Using Crystals, Color, Aromatherapy & the Power of Positive Thought.* Woodbury, MN: Llewellyn Publications, 2011.

———. *Color Your Life with Crystals: Your First Guide to Crystals, Colors and Chakras*. Rochester, VT: Earthdancer Books. 2013.

———. *Crystal Intentions Oracle: Guidance & Affirmations*. Woodbury, MN: Llewellyn Publications, 2016.

———. *The Essential Guide to Crystals, Minerals and Stones*. Woodbury, MN: Llewellyn Publications, 2013.

———. *The Essential Guide to Aromatherapy and Vibrational Healing*. Woodbury, MN: Llewellyn Publications, 2016.

———. *Masters, Mystics, Saints and Gemstone Guardians Cards*. Forres, Scotland: Findhorn Press, 2017.

———. *Gemstone Guardians Cards and Your Soul Purpose*. Rochester, VT: Findhorn Press, 2020.

Marciniak, Barbara. *Earth: Pleiadian Keys to the Living Library*. Rochester, VT: Bear & Company, 1995.

Melody. *Love is in the Earth: A Kaleidoscope of Crystals*. Wheat Ridge, CO: Earth-Love, 1991.

Milanovich, Norma, and Shirley McCune. *The Light Shall Set You Free*. Kalispell, MT: Athena Publishing, 1996.

Raphaell, Katrina. *Crystal Enlightenment: The Transforming Properties of Crystals and Healing Stones*. Santa Fe, NM: Aurora Press, 1985.

———. *Crystal Healing: The Therapeutic Application of Crystals and Stones*. Santa Fe, NM: Aurora Press, 1987.

———. *The Crystalline Transmission: A Synthesis of Light*. Santa Fe, NM: Aurora Press, 1990.

Raven, Hazel. *The Secrets of Angel Healing: Therapies for Mind, Body and Spirit*. London: Godsfield, 2006.

Sellar, Wanda. *The Directory of Essential Oils*. Ashingdon, England: C.W. Daniel, 1992.

Sams, Jamie. *The 13 Original Clan Mothers: Your Sacred Path to Discovering the Gifts, Talents, & Abilities of the Feminine Through the Ancient Teachings of the Sisterhood.* New York: Harper San Francisco, 1993.

Shapiro, Rami. *The Angelic Way: Angels through the Ages and Their Meanings for Us.* New York: Blue Bridge Books, 2009.

Stein, Diane. *The Women's Book of Healing.* St. Paul, MN: Llewellyn Publications, 1987.

Taylor, Terry Lynn. *Messengers of Light: The Angels' Guide to Spiritual Growth.* Tiburon, CA: HJ Kramer, 1989.

Tisserand, Robert, and Rodney Young. *Essential Oil Safety: A Guide for Health Care Professionals.* 2nd ed. London: Churchill Livingstone Elsevier, 2014.

Tompkins, Peter, and Christopher Bird. *The Secret Life of Plants.* New York: Harper, 1989.

Waters, Frank. *Book of the Hopi.* New York: Penguin Books, 1977.

White Eagle. *Spiritual Unfoldment 2.* Liss, England: White Eagle Publishing Trust, 2008.

Worwood, Susan, and Valerie Ann Worwood. *Essential Aromatherapy: A Pocket Guide to Essential Oils and Aromatherapy.* Novato, CA: New World Library, 1995.

Shinn, Florence Scovel. *The Writings of Florence Scovel Shinn.* Camarillo, CA: DeVorss, 1996.

Webster, Richard. *Encyclopedia of Angels.* Woodbury, MN: Llewellyn Publications, 2012. Kindle.

Yogananda, Parmahansa. *Autobiography of a Yogi.* Nevada City, CA: Crystal Clarity, 2005.

INDEX

B

C

Q

S

To Write to the Author

If you wish to contact the author or would like more information about this book, please write to the author in care of Llewellyn Worldwide Ltd. and we will forward your request. Both the author and publisher appreciate hearing from you and learning of your enjoyment of this book and how it has helped you. Llewellyn Worldwide Ltd. cannot guarantee that every letter written to the author can be answered, but all will be forwarded. Please write to:

Margaret Ann Lembo
℅ Llewellyn Worldwide
2143 Wooddale Drive
Woodbury, MN 55125-2989

Please enclose a self-addressed stamped envelope for reply,
or $1.00 to cover costs. If outside the U.S.A., enclose
an international postal reply coupon.

Many of Llewellyn's authors have websites with additional information and resources. For more information, please visit our website at http://www.llewellyn.com